Religion
in
America

Opposing Viewpoints®

Religion
in
America

Opposing Viewpoints®

Other Books of Related Interest

Religion in America

Opposing Viewpoints®

William Dudley, *Book Editor*

Bonnie Szumski, *Editorial Director*
Scott Barbour, *Managing Editor*

OPPOSING
VIEWPOINTS®
SERIES

Greenhaven Press, Inc., San Diego, California

Cover photo: Corbis Images, Inc.

Library of Congress Cataloging-in-Publication Data

Religion in America: opposing viewpoints / William Dudley,
book editor.
   p. cm. — (Opposing viewpoints series)
   Includes bibliographical references and index.
   ISBN 1-56510-002-6 (pbk. : alk. paper) —
ISBN 1-56510-003-4 (lib. bdg. : alk. paper)
   1. United States—Religion. I. Dudley, William, 1964–
II. Opposing viewpoints series (Unnumbered)

BL2525 .R465 2002
200'.973—dc21
                                                      2001018806
                                                             CIP

Greenhaven Press, Inc., P.O. Box 289009
San Diego, CA 92198-9009

"Congress shall make no law. . .abridging the freedom of speech, or of the press."

First Amendment to the U.S. Constitution

The basic foundation of our democracy is the First Amendment guarantee of freedom of expression. The Opposing Viewpoints Series is dedicated to the concept of this basic freedom and the idea that it is more important to practice it than to enshrine it.

Contents

Why Consider Opposing Viewpoints?

"The only way in which a human being can make some approach to knowing the whole of a subject is by hearing what can be said about it by persons of every variety of opinion and studying all modes in which it can be looked at by every character of mind. No wise man ever acquired his wisdom in any mode but this."

John Stuart Mill

In our media-intensive culture it is not difficult to find differing opinions. Thousands of newspapers and magazines and dozens of radio and television talk shows resound with differing points of view. The difficulty lies in deciding which opinion to agree with and which "experts" seem the most credible. The more inundated we become with differing opinions and claims, the more essential it is to hone critical reading and thinking skills to evaluate these ideas. Opposing Viewpoints books address this problem directly by presenting stimulating debates that can be used to enhance and teach these skills. The varied opinions contained in each book examine many different aspects of a single issue. While examining these conveniently edited opposing views, readers can develop critical thinking skills such as the ability to compare and contrast authors' credibility, facts, argumentation styles, use of persuasive techniques, and other stylistic tools. In short, the Opposing Viewpoints Series is an ideal way to attain the higher-level thinking and reading skills so essential in a culture of diverse and contradictory opinions.

In addition to providing a tool for critical thinking, Opposing Viewpoints books challenge readers to question their own strongly held opinions and assumptions. Most people form their opinions on the basis of upbringing, peer pressure, and personal, cultural, or professional bias. By reading carefully balanced opposing views, readers must directly confront new ideas as well as the opinions of those with whom they disagree. This is not to simplistically argue that everyone who reads opposing views will—or should—change his or her opinion. Instead, the series enhances readers' understanding of their own views by encouraging confrontation with opposing ideas. Careful examination of others' views can lead to the readers' understanding of the logical inconsistencies in their own opinions, perspective on why they hold an opinion, and the consideration of the possibility that their opinion requires further evaluation.

Evaluating Other Opinions

To ensure that this type of examination occurs, Opposing Viewpoints books present all types of opinions. Prominent spokespeople on different sides of each issue as well as well-known professionals from many disciplines challenge the reader. An additional goal of the series is to provide a forum for other, less known, or even unpopular viewpoints. The opinion of an ordinary person who has had to make the decision to cut off life support from a terminally ill relative, for example, may be just as valuable and provide just as much insight as a medical ethicist's professional opinion. The editors have two additional purposes in including these less known views. One, the editors encourage readers to respect others' opinions—even when not enhanced by professional credibility. It is only by reading or listening to and objectively evaluating others' ideas that one can determine whether they are worthy of consideration. Two, the inclusion of such viewpoints encourages the important critical thinking skill of objectively evaluating an author's credentials and bias. This evaluation will illuminate an author's reasons for taking a particular stance on an issue and will aid in readers' evaluation of the author's ideas.

It is our hope that these books will give readers a deeper understanding of the issues debated and an appreciation of the complexity of even seemingly simple issues when good and honest people disagree. This awareness is particularly important in a democratic society such as ours in which people enter into public debate to determine the common good. Those with whom one disagrees should not be regarded as enemies but rather as people whose views deserve careful examination and may shed light on one's own.

Thomas Jefferson once said that "difference of opinion leads to inquiry, and inquiry to truth." Jefferson, a broadly educated man, argued that "if a nation expects to be ignorant and free . . . it expects what never was and never will be." As individuals and as a nation, it is imperative that we consider the opinions of others and examine them with skill and discernment. The Opposing Viewpoints Series is intended to help readers achieve this goal.

David L. Bender and Bruno Leone,
Founders

Greenhaven Press anthologies primarily consist of previously published material taken from a variety of sources, including periodicals, books, scholarly journals, newspapers, government documents, and position papers from private and public organizations. These original sources are often edited for length and to ensure their accessibility for a young adult audience. The anthology editors also change the original titles of these works in order to clearly present the main thesis of each viewpoint and to explicitly indicate the opinion presented in the viewpoint. These alterations are made in consideration of both the reading and comprehension levels of a young adult audience. Every effort is made to ensure that Greenhaven Press accurately reflects the original intent of the authors included in this anthology.

Introduction

"Religion, faith, and morality are deeply private things, and should remain that way."

—Philadelphia Daily News

"The separation of church and state prohibits the establishment of a state religion. But it does not demand that religion be limited to the private side of life."

—Kenneth L. Woodward

In 2000, Democratic Party presidential candidate Al Gore picked Connecticut senator Joseph Lieberman to be his running mate, making Lieberman the first Jewish American to be a major party candidate for vice president. Although Gore and Lieberman were not ultimately elected, Lieberman's presence in the presidential race renewed perennial debates as to the proper place of religion in American life and politics.

Lieberman, a religiously observant member of the Orthodox branch of Judaism, raised the issue of religion in America in several well-publicized campaign speeches and pronouncements. In a noted speech at the University of Notre Dame, a Roman Catholic institution, he called for increasing religion's role in the public realm. Lieberman argued that America was founded on a moral consensus that was rooted in religious values. The people who led the American Revolution and wrote the Constitution "were men of profound faith and recognized as such the necessity of religion in a free society," he claimed. America's founders believed that

> in a democratic state with limited power, religion, while not the only source, was certainly a most powerful source of values and good behavior. The core of these original values— faith, family, and freedom, equal opportunity, respect for the basic dignity of human life, and tolerance for individual differences—clearly had their roots in the Judeo-Christian ethic of the Founders. . . . Over the years they evolved into an American civic religion—deistic, principled, purposeful, moral, public, and not least of all, inclusive—a civic religion that . . . made real the ideal of *E pluribus unum*, from many, one.

14

But America's core values, Lieberman believes, have been muffled in contemporary times because of a growing "ambivalence" towards religious faith and its private and public roles. "We have not abandoned our individual belief in those first principles," he noted in his Notre Dame address. "But we have grown increasingly unwilling to embrace and act on them publicly and collectively." Because of this, "we have practically banished religious values and religious institutions from the public square and constructed a 'discomfort zone' for even discussing our faith in public settings." As a result, Lieberman asserted, America is experiencing broken families, schoolyard violence, a depraved popular culture, and other disturbing social trends. "We must rebuild our moral consensus," he concluded. "We must take our religious beliefs and values—our sense of justice, of right or wrong—into America's cultural and communal life."

Not everyone agreed with Lieberman's call for a stronger public role for religion. The Anti-Defamation League (ADL), a Jewish civil rights organization, wrote an open letter to Lieberman that stated: "Appealing along religious lines, or belief in God, is contrary to the American ideal. . . . Public profession of religious beliefs should not be an elemental part of . . . any political campaign." For the ADL and other critics, American democracy *and* healthy religious life are dependent on religion staying out of the public sphere. They note that when America became independent from England, the former colonies not only broke away from its government, but also from the official Church of England. Rather than create a national church of its own, America's founders instead explicitly forbade any "religious test" for public office and included religious freedom as the first civil liberty listed in the Bill of Rights. Cultural critic Ellen Willis expresses the view shared by many who believe that religion should remain a private rather than a public matter:

> I believe that a democratic polity requires a secular state: one that does not fund or otherwise sponsor religious institutions and activities. . . . Furthermore, a genuinely democratic society requires a secular ethos: one that does not equate morality with religion, stigmatize atheists, defer to religious interests and aims over others or make religious beliefs an informal qualification for public office.

A central concern raised by those who oppose a stronger public role for religion is that such a development would result in the official endorsement of a majority religion to the detriment of minority faiths. Journalist Katha Pollitt argues that "bringing religion into the public sphere in practice simply means that the biggest and best organized religion gets to use the public realm—public facilities, public money—to advance its own agenda." Indeed, for much of America's history, Christianity in some form has been the dominant religion in America.

However, in recent decades both immigration and changing belief patterns have greatly increased religious diversity in America, with Islam, Buddhism, and other religions and belief systems gaining many adherents. *Washington Post* columnist E.J. Dionne argues that Lieberman's willingness to speak out on his religious faith, despite his status as a member of a minority religion (Jews make up about 2 percent of the adult American population), represents a national triumph of religious diversity and toleration: "We've passed from a time when Protestantism provided the dominant language of public faith in our country. Now, people of other faiths can invoke their religion in a political campaign and be accepted, even praised."

The place of religion in America's public realm, including government programs and public schools, is one of many contentious issues examined in *Religion in America: Opposing Viewpoints*. Contributors provide a diversity of views on both the private religious attitudes of Americans and on the social role of religious belief in the following chapters: Is America a Religious Nation? Can Religion Solve America's Social Problems? What Should Be Done to Accommodate Religious Freedom in America? What Role Should Religion Play in America's Public Schools? This sampling of contemporary debates illustrates how religion is both a divisive and unifying force in American society.

Chapter Preface

Scholars and observers who attempt to determine whether America is a religious nation are confronted with the challenge of having no definitive measure of "religiosity." Some commonly cited points of evidence, such as opinion surveys and rates of religious service attendance, may be less revealing than they first seem.

As measured by responses to public opinion polls, the importance of religion in America is at first glance hard to deny. According to Gallup Organization surveys, 95 percent of Americans believe in God—a number that has remained remarkably consistent over the decades and that is much higher than in other industrialized countries (comparable polls show 76 percent of people in Britain professing belief in God, and 52 percent in Sweden). Yet for some, such poll results do not constitute an adequate gauge of religious faith of individuals or what religion means to America as a nation. People who profess a belief in God may differ greatly on how important religion is in their lives. They may have very different conceptions of what God is—an all-knowing deity who created and rules the universe, a spirit or life force, or a state of higher human consciousness. "To put it succinctly," writes public opinion analyst George Bishop, "when Americans say they believe in God . . . there may not be wide agreement among them in what they mean by 'God' nor in how certain they are of what they believe."

Another possible measure of religiosity in America is religious service attendance. Since the 1930s, the percentage of Americans who tell pollsters that they attended religious services in a given week has remained steady at about 40 percent—again, a much higher rate than Britain (10 percent) and Scandinavia (4 percent). Most sociologists of religion have agreed that, while specific denominations have fallen and risen in popularity, overall worship attendance has remained constant, indicating that America is a religious nation.

However, some scholars of American religion have wondered whether the reported rates of organized religious activity were accurate—in other words, whether Americans who claimed to regularly attend church actually did so. In the early 1990s three sociologists, C. Kirk Hadaway, Penny Long Marler, and Mark Chaves, did an intensive study of church attendance in a county in Ohio. They concluded that while 36 percent of county residents claimed to go to church weekly, their head count revealed that only 19.6 percent actually showed up at services. "We have shown that the church attendance rate is probably one-half what everyone thinks it is," they concluded. Other sociologists have since criticized their methodology and conclusions, leaving the real rate of U.S. worship attendance shrouded in uncertainty.

The above examples illustrate some of the complexities that arise when trying to determine what role religion has in American life. The viewpoints that follow provide differing perspectives on aspects of this question.

"America's founding fathers expected our nation to be (on the whole) Christian, and our government to reflect that bias."

America Was Founded on Christian Principles

Summit Ministries

Arguments over whether the United States is a religious nation often focus on its history. Many people believe that America has rejected the religious (specifically Christian) ideals that were present at the nation's founding. Such a contention appears in the following viewpoint by Summit Ministries, a Christian ministry and educational organization. The group asserts that America's founders—the people who fought the American Revolution and wrote the U.S. Constitution—acted on the assumption that America was and would continue to be a predominantly Christian country. However, modern judicial interpretations of the Constitution have established a wall of separation of church and state and effectively banished religion from public affairs in America. This, according to the ministry, created a spiritual void that enabled the values of "Secular Humanism" to dominate American schools and governments. America must choose to once again acknowledge God as the supreme authority, the organization concludes.

As you read, consider the following questions:
1. What was the true intention of the religion clause in the First Amendment, according to Summit Ministries?
2. What does Summit Ministries find objectionable about "Secular Humanism"?

Reprinted, with permission, from "The Role of the Bible and Christianity in America," by Summit Ministries, *Christian Answers Network*, as found at the following URL: www.ChristianAnswers.net/q-sum/sum-g001.html (as downloaded 9/27/00).

The Bible, and Christian principles in general, are being censored from our public schools—in fact, from the whole "public square." Under the guise of adhering to the "separation of church and state doctrine," judges and other government officials are disallowing Christianity in the growing number of arenas administered by the United States government. The censorship is swift and complete, effectively compartmentalizing the church's influence in the world. As [law professor] John Eidsmoe says, "Those who object to Christian expression in public life frequently use the phrase as a code-word to mean, separation of church from reality. They say, 'Christians can stay in church and pray and sing, but leave the real problems of the world to us.'"

As Christians, we realize that the real problems of the world can only be solved with reference to Biblical Christian principles. But recently Christians have been told that such an attitude is "unconstitutional"; that the First Amendment to the United States Constitution includes a clause that calls for the separation of church and state. Many people now espouse the belief that American government was designed to include "an impenetrable wall" separating church and state. If this is true, then the Christian is violating the founding principles of our country when he or she calls for Christianity to be voiced in the public square. But is it true?

The First Amendment

Absolutely not. The First Amendment does not include the phrase "separation of church and state." It reads: "Congress shall make no law respecting an establishment of religion, or prohibiting the free exercise thereof; or abridging the freedom of speech, or of the press; or the right of the people peaceably to assemble, and to petition the Government for a redress of grievances." Nowhere does the First Amendment suggest that Christianity cannot be heard in the public square.

[Political scientist] Robert L. Cord accurately describes the true intention of the religion clause in the First Amendment: "[R]egarding religion, the First Amendment was intended to accomplish three purposes. First, it was intended to prevent the establishment of a national church or religion, or the giving of any religious sect or denomination a preferred status. Second, it was designed to safeguard the right of freedom of conscience in religious beliefs against invasion solely by the national Government. Third, it was so constructed in order to allow the States, unimpeded, to deal with religious establishments and aid to religious institutions as they saw fit." The founding fathers did not include the First Amendment in the Constitution to disallow Christianity from influencing state-established institutions; on the contrary, America's founding fathers expected our nation to be (on the whole) Christian, and our government to reflect that bias.

The Faith of America's Founders

When our founders talked religiously about politics they borrowed mostly from the Jewish Testament, not the Christian. Scholars often mistakenly refer to the God of the founders as a deist god. But the founders talked about God in terms that are radically Jewish: Creator, Judge, and Providence. These were the names they most commonly used for him, notably in the Declaration of Independence. For the most part, these are not names that could have come from the Greeks or Romans but only from the Jewish Testament. Perhaps the founders avoided Christian language to avert divisiveness, since different colonies were founded under different Christian inspirations. All found common language in the language of the Jewish Testament.

If I stress the religious elements of the story, it is because for the past century scholars have paid too much attention to [Thomas] Jefferson in these matters and ignored the other top one hundred founders, most of whom were profoundly religious men. The crucial point is that *all* the Founding Fathers—Jefferson included—shared in common a belief that a people cannot maintain liberty without religion. They understood the power of religion to their cause yet worried that in the eyes of God they would be found wanting.

Michael Novak, *Hoover Digest*, Spring 2000.

This appears to be a reasonable understanding of the First Amendment—far more reasonable than asserting that it erected an impenetrable wall of separation. And it becomes even more reasonable when one considers the words and actions of America's settlers, founders and leaders.

The first act of the United States Congress was to authorize the printing of 20,000 Bibles for the Indians. Further, "When our first President, under the new Constitution, received the request of both Houses of Congress concerning a national declaration of a public day of Thanksgiving and Prayer, 'George Washington . . . issued a National Thanksgiving Proclamation' without any apparent concern that he might be mixing government and religion." The men who founded our country clearly wedded it to Christian principles. "By today's standards," as syndicated columnist Don Feder says, "the founding fathers were the religious right."

[Author] Tim LaHaye says that "This Christian consensus is easily verified by the fact that prior to 1789 (the year that eleven of the thirteen states ratified the Constitution), many of the states still had constitutional requirements that a man must be a Christian in order to hold public office." This Christian consensus was understood by leaders long after the American Revolution, as well. Abraham Lincoln, in 1863, called for a "National Fast Day," citing the fact that "We have been the recipients of the choicest bounties of Heaven. . . . But we have forgotten God."

Secular Humanism Fills the Vacuum

When one examines history, one cannot avoid the conclusion that America was founded on Christian principles and the assumption that her citizenry would adhere to those same principles. Unfortunately, the modern interpretation of the First Amendment ignores historical fact. Instead, it provides a convenient vehicle for Secular Humanism to achieve control over the public square. The reason for this is simple: there is no such thing as a value-free society or institution—someone's values must prevail. Some worldview must "fill the vacuum" left by the eradication of the Christian worldview from public education, social services, courtrooms, etc. By distorting the First Amendment, the United States government has allowed Humanist values to prevail. As LaHaye points out, "The true meaning of the first amendment has been turned on its head during the past fifty years: In this decade, those who practice the religion of secular humanism are able to use the power of the federal government to impose their religion on the vast majority of the population."

The danger of Secular Humanism prevailing in our society is, quite simply, the oldest danger recorded in the Bible: men setting themselves up as God. The moral framework of our universe guarantees terrible consequences for the country that grants sovereignty to something other than God—because in such circumstances sovereignty ultimately becomes the property of the state. "Man is a spiritual being," says [author] Benjamin Hart. "When one faith is eliminated, a new god will rush in to fill the spiritual void. Throughout history, there has been a man-made god called the state." When the state holds ultimate authority, government officials may commit whatever atrocities they like, because only the state may determine what is right and wrong.

America's Choice

America must choose. Either we ignore the intentions of our founding fathers and grant sovereignty to the state (clearing the way for Hitlers and Stalins to reign once again), or we bow humbly before the one true God, and—without establishing Christianity as the mandatory religion for all citizens—obey God's principles for justice. True freedom can only exist in a land governed according to the principles set forth in Romans 13:3–4: "For rulers hold no terror for those who do right, but for those who do wrong. Do you want to be free from fear of the one in authority? Then do what is right and he will commend you. For he is God's servant to do you good. But if you do wrong, be afraid, for he does not bear the sword for nothing. He is God's servant, an agent of wrath to bring punishment on the wrong-doer."

> "The Constitution is a 'Godless document,' a fact that was immediately evident to evangelical Christians of the constitutional era."

America Was Not Founded on Christian Principles

Mark Weldon Whitten

Mark Weldon Whitten is a college philosophy and religion instructor. In the following viewpoint, he refutes the argument that the United States was founded as a Christian nation. Whitten examines historical evidence, including the text of the Constitution, and concludes that the nation's founders intended to establish a national government based on the principle that church and state should be wholly separate.

As you read, consider the following questions:
1. What arguments does Whitten make to explain the absence of the words "separation of church and state" in the Constitution?
2. What are the seven main points of evidence that the author uses to support his argument that church-state separation was fundamental constitutional principle?
3. What does separation of church and state mean, according to Whitten?

Reprinted, with permission, from "Was America Founded as a 'Christian Nation'?" by Mark Weldon Whitten, *Human Quest*, May/June 1999.

It has often been charged that America was founded as a 'Christian nation' and that separation of church and state is a 'lie' or a 'myth,' because it is not 'in' the Constitution of the United States. How accurate are such judgments?

As a matter of fact, the words 'separation of church and state' are not contained in the text of the Constitution. Yet, the words 'separation of powers' are also not found in the text of the Constitution—but who could competently argue that the separation of powers is not a constitutional doctrine?

Members of the Religious Right who reject church-state separation are predominantly Christian trinitarian theists, yet the word 'trinity' is not found in the Bible. Do they, therefore, wish to deny that trinitarianism is a biblical doctrine?

The real issue is not whether the words 'separation of church and state' are found in the text of the Constitution, but whether the principle of church-state separation is a constitutional assumption and principle, and what church-state separation actually means and entails.

Seven Evidences

Seven decisive evidences demonstrate that church-state separation is a constitutional assumption and principle. One such evidence consists in the fact that no theological or biblical arguments, and no prayers for divine guidance or approval, were offered during the Constitutional Convention of 1787, contrary to what contemporary myth-makers like [author and speaker] David Barton have irresponsibly asserted. . . .

A second evidence consists of the fact that the text of the Constitution makes no appeals to religious authorities, rationales, or purposes. The Constitution is a 'Godless document,' a fact that was immediately evident to evangelical Christians of the constitutional era. Timothy Dwight, evangelical president of Yale University declared:

> The nation has offended Providence. We formed our constitution without any acknowledgment of God; without any recognition of his mercies to us as a people, of his government or even of his existence. The [constitutional] convention by which it was formed, never asked, even once, his direction, or his blessings, upon their labors. Thus we commenced our national existence under the present system without God.

A third evidence that church-state separation is a constitutional principle consists of the fact that Article VI, Section III of the Constitution—the only substantive mention of religion in the Constitution—prohibits any religious tests for holding political office. It was rightly recognized by most (and wrongly objected to by many) at the time that this restriction allowed anyone of whatever religion, or none at all, to serve in the federal government. . . .

A Misunderstood Biblical Passage

Many well-intentioned Christians have been misled in recent years into equating their country with the kingdom of God. They have been told the United States must turn back to God or face doom. Scripture is misused and misapplied, particularly Old Testament passages dealing with Israel, so that America is seen as a covenant nation.

The most widely misinterpreted passage is 2 Chronicles 7:14, which reads:

> If my people, which are called by my name, shall humble themselves, and pray, and seek my face, and turn from their wicked ways; then will I hear from heaven, and will forgive their sin, and will heal their land. (King James Version)

The problem with taking such a passage and applying it to America—or to any other nation—is that it overlooks the New Testament's clear teaching that God's new nation—his new people—is the church. God's ancient covenant with his people Israel, Paul's letters and Hebrews teach, has been replaced by a new covenant with the church of Jesus Christ.

Yet, some religious leaders point again and again to this one verse from 2 Chronicles in making the argument that if America is to continue as God's chosen nation, it must repent and return to him.

Baptist Joint Committee on Public Affairs, "Christianity in American Life," 1996.

A fourth evidence that church-state separation is a constitutional principle consists of the fact that the *Federalist Papers*—written by Alexander Hamilton, James Madison, and John Jay to 'sell' the new Constitution to the American people—also made no appeal to religious authorities, rationales, or purposes to legitimize the Constitution. . . .

Madison's Views

Fifth of all, while it is true that Thomas Jefferson, who wrote the letter to Danbury Baptists which contains the phrase 'wall of separation,' was not a member of the Constitutional Convention, James Madison was. Madison was the most influential member of the Constitutional Convention and was the driving force behind the creation and adoption of the Bill of Rights, including the First Amendment with its guarantees of free exercise and non-establishment of religion. Madison as president practiced a quite strict separation of church and state. Madison wrote:

> There remains . . . a strong bias toward the old error, that without some sort of alliance or coalition between government and religion neither can be duly supported. Such indeed is the tendency to such a coalition, and such is its corrupting influence on the parties, that the danger cannot be too carefully guarded. . . . Every new and successful example of a perfect separation between ecclesiastical and civil matters is of importance. . . . And I have no doubt that every new example will succeed, as every past one has done, in showing that religion and government will both exist in greater purity, the less they are mixed together. . . .

Sixth, the debate in the First congress on the wording of the First Amendment demonstrates that it was designed and understood to disallow not only particular and preferential aid to one Christian denomination over others, but also non-preferential aid to religion in general. Wording that would have allowed non-preferential aid to Christian denominations in general was carefully considered and rejected. . . .

Separation of Church and State

Finally, the text of the First Amendment itself refutes the idea that it does not embody the principle of church-state separation. As Justice Wiley Rutledge incisively and decisively wrote in the Supreme Court decision *Zorach vs. Clauson* (1947):

> The amendment's purpose was not to strike merely at the official establishment of a single sect, creed, or religion. . . . The object was broader than separation of church and state in the narrow sense. . . . 'Religion' appears only once in the amendment. But the word governs two prohibitions and it governs them alike. It does not have two meanings, one narrow to forbid an 'establishment' and another, much broader,

for securing 'the free exercise thereof.' Congress and now the states are as broadly restricted concerning the one as they are the other.

Government cannot make any law respecting an establishment of religion—any and all religions! Nor can government prohibit the free exercise of religion—any and all religions! And no religion can use its political influence upon government to establish itself socially in a favored position over other religions. That is separation of church and state.

"*By all the normal yardsticks of religious
commitment . . . the United States has
resisted the pressures toward secularity.*"

Americans Are a
Religious People

Kenneth D. Wald

Kenneth D. Wald is a professor of political science at the
University of Florida, Gainesville. He has written and contributed to numerous books on religion and politics, including *Religion and Politics in the United States*, from which the
following viewpoint is excerpted. Wald asserts that religion
remains an important force in the United States as measured
by church attendance, surveys on religious beliefs, and other
indicators. The vast majority of Americans profess belief in
the central assumptions of Christianity in particular, including belief in God, the divinity of Jesus, and the reality of life
after death. The vitality of religion in America disproves the
hypothesis that religion inevitably declines as a society un-
dergoes modernization, Wald contends.

As you read, consider the following questions:
1. What "naive understanding" of secularization does Wald
   argue is proven invalid by the American experience?
2. What yardsticks does the author use to measure religious
   commitment in America?
3. What insights does Wald take from sociological studies
   of Muncie, Indiana?

B y most conventional yardsticks, the United States was one of the first nations to have undergone modernization, and it continues to lead the way in many aspects of social development. If modernization leads inevitably to the decline of religious institutions, practices, and feelings—what I have called the "naive" understanding of secularization—then the erosion of religion ought to show up first in such a mobile, affluent, urban, and expansive society. Yet American religion, like Mark Twain, has obstinately refused to comply with reports of its demise.

American religion has certainly experienced the processes associated with the neutral definition of secularization. Religion is a specialized institution with a limited public role and religious affiliation is a matter of personal choice. Consistent with the experience of desacralization, Americans generally interpret events from a scientific and naturalist perspective. Many orthodox doctrines and forms of devotion have been abandoned or modified by church authorities. But these changes do not add up to the global decline in faith predicted by naive secularization theory. It cannot be denied that some religions have lost intensity, esteem, and membership or that many Americans are indifferent or antagonistic toward religion. Yet even these elements of decline have been offset by spectacular growth in some religions, the flowering of new faiths, periodic revivals of religious enthusiasm, and the spread of religious sentiment to some of the most "secularized" segments of the population. The naive model of secularization cannot withstand the facts. . . .

By all the normal yardsticks of religious commitment—the strength of religious institutions, practices, and belief—the United States has resisted the pressures toward secularity. Institutionally, churches are probably the most vital voluntary organization in a country that puts a premium on "joining up." There are between 255,000 and 300,000 churches in the United States with a total membership of about 137 million. Depending on how "membership" is defined, the church members amount to somewhere between three-fifths and three-fourths of the adult population. Despite all the talk about "decline," the proportion of church members among persons aged fifteen and older is virtually the same today as it was in 1950 and, with due allowance for the raggedness of historical data, actually seems to be higher now than throughout most of American history. High as it is, the proportion of church membership may understate the full extent of American religious consciousness. Even if they are not affiliated with any religious organization, nine out of ten Americans typically claim to identify with some religious group or tradition.

Support for organized religion shows up in other ways. In annual surveys about confidence in major institutions, churches and organized religion have consistently been ranked at or near the top of the list. Along the same lines, the clergy has regularly outdistanced almost all other occupational groups in public estimates of honesty and ethical standards. This vote of confidence has been backed up by perhaps the ultimate expression of commitment—the pocketbook. In 1986, for example, Americans contributed more than $40 billion to religious institutions, making churches by far the most favored recipient of philanthropy. Congregations devoted a significant share of that income to education, human service, health and hospitals, community development, the arts, and environmental protection. With its $1.5 billion annual budget, Catholic Charities is second only to the U.S. government in welfare activities, and the number of Americans working abroad for Christian organizations dwarfs the number of civilian U.S. government employees stationed abroad.

Religious Behaviors

Surveys of church practice, another presumed casualty of the modern age, show an equally high level of attachment to religion. What anthropologists call "rites of passage" (formal celebrations of an individual's progress through life, such as naming ceremonies, attainment of adulthood, marriage, and funerals) are still monopolized by the churches in the United States, as they are in many other cultures. But as national data reveal, devotion is hardly limited to such occasions (see fig. 1). At one extreme, about one-third of the population claims never to attend church outside of weddings and funerals. The "unchurched" comprise the self-defined irreligious (9 percent of the entire population), another 7 percent who consider themselves religious but who have no denom-

Figure 1

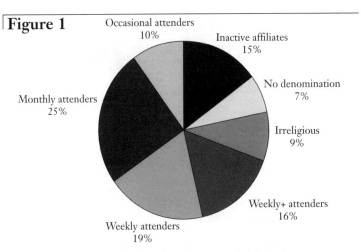

Frequency of Churchgoing in the United States

Calculated by the author from the 1989 pilot study, American National Election Study, Center for Political Studies.

inational commitment, and the remaining 15 percent who identify personally with a religious group but do not participate. Slightly more than one-third of the population maintains a moderate association with churches. Though the moderate category includes those who attend church only a few times a year (10 percent), most people in this category (25 percent) attend at least once a month. The most intensely religious third of the population includes people who are in church every week (19 percent) and those who attend even more than once a week (16 percent).

Churchgoing is but one form of religious behavior; Americans engage in a wide range of other public and private devotional acts (see fig. 2). More than three-quarters of all Americans identify with a religion and consider it important in their lives. Substantial majorities report formal membership in a church and daily prayers. Approximately one-third of the population claims to get a "great deal" of daily guidance from religion and to monitor religious television and radio programs weekly. Almost 20 percent say they read the Bible on a daily basis. One in ten claims membership in independent religious organizations and daily reading about religion in newspapers and magazines. About one in twenty

Figure 2

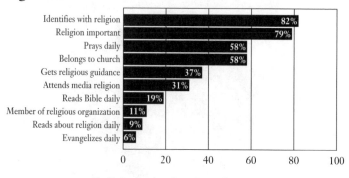

Religiosity in the United States

Calculated by the author from the 1989 pilot study, American National Election Study, Center for Political Studies.

report attempting to convince someone else to accept their faith each day. Based on questions from the same survey, religious involvement appears far more widespread than many forms of political participation. More Americans identify with a denomination than a political party, and the typical citizen is much more likely to attend church than a political meeting. The proportion of citizens who claim to evangelize on behalf of their faith exceeds the percentage who report having tried to influence another person's vote.

A Shell of Religion?

But do these findings refer merely to the shell of religion and mask weaknesses in the power exerted by religious values? Certainly the American people believe religion is losing influence in society, and external critics regard the statistics as superficial, a tribute more to habit and conformity than to deep-seated faith. In truth, it is much more challenging to prove the persistence of religious feeling. Precisely that aspect of religion—its capacity to keep people's minds focused on questions of ultimate value, on heaven, hell, right, wrong, judgment, justice—should have declined with the triumph of modern culture. Because feelings of any sort are notoriously slippery things to measure, perhaps the best that can be done here is to note that major studies of contemporary values

34

have repeatedly asserted the underlying importance of religion. For example, a major life insurance company commissioned a report to assess what Americans believed and how those beliefs were related to factors such as age, social standing, place of residence, and so forth. Despite this secular orientation, the authors found that the religious factor emerged as a kind of superstar among all the other pieces of information: "In investigating major aspects of American life—community involvement, political and moral beliefs, personal relationships, and work—time and again, systematic analysis led to the one factor that consistently and dramatically affects the values and behavior of Americans. This factor is level of religious commitment. The initial intention of this study was not to prepare a report on the impact of religion on American life, but the pattern of responses was compelling."

Detailed findings from a host of surveys have borne out this conclusion. By overwhelming majorities, Americans have continued to endorse the core assumptions of Christianity—the existence of God, the divinity of Jesus, the reality of an afterlife—and to insist on the importance of these values in their own lives. Most Americans believe in the divine origins of humankind and nearly a majority accept a literal interpretation of the Genesis story. When Americans think about God, they conceive of a creator and healer; the image of heaven carried in the minds of modern Americans depicts a place of union with God and reunion with loved ones. "Two centuries after the intellectual world has said that these kinds of things do not happen," reported a scholar who interviewed two thousand small-town Midwesterners, "many people reported mystical experiences such as visions, prophetic dreams, voices from heaven, and visits from spirits." Despite all the publicity accorded the "New Age" movement, Americans are much more likely to perceive a spirit world of angels and devils than to believe in crystals and channeling and may in fact be less disposed today to believe in magic and astrology than they were centuries ago.

To the extent that such things can be measured, religious feeling, like religious institutions and practices, has survived intact in probably the most "modern" society known in history. Statistics have been used to make the point because numbers are the currency of argument in a scientific culture. But because national statistics often have a numbing effect, they should be supplemented with a local example. The stability of a religious texture in American life has been demonstrated forcefully by a continuing study of a small industrial town in eastern Indiana. In the 1920s a pair of gifted social observers decided to put "Middletown," a pseudonym for Muncie, under the microscope of social analysis. Curious about the changes wrought by the passage of fifty years, a team of social scientists set out in the 1970s to repeat the study of Muncie. In the half-century since the first study, Muncie had experienced all the changes that are supposed to encourage secularization—rapid population growth, relentless technological advance, the spread of education, increasing bureaucracy, the penetration of mass media, an expanded governmental presence. Could the vibrant religious tradition of the town possibly survive the corrosive effects of these changes?

Despite the odds against it, traditional religion was found to be doing quite nicely in modern Muncie. In the words of the most recent (1983) study of the town, "The Reverend Rip Van Winkle, Methodist minister, awakening in Middletown after a 60-year sleep, would hardly know he had been away." He might be surprised by the growth of tolerance among religious groups, but little else had changed since the 1920s. The "Middletown" residents of the 1970s seemed every bit as pious as their grandparents and great-grandparents. Most people still subscribed to the core beliefs of Christianity and, whether measured by the numbers of clergy and buildings, by financial contributions, or by attendance at worship, the churches flourished. But surely, it may be argued, the survival of religion was purchased at a high price—by sacrificing the traditional emphasis on the emotional and spiritual for a more modern style stressing reason and social reform. This plausible suggestion collapses under the evidence of growth in the most theologically conservative churches, a renewed emphasis on emotional forms of worship in all denominations, and the continuing priority placed by the clergy on the spiritual well-being of their flocks. Against all expectations, the most recent study of Muncie uncovered a community with reverence for the sacred and faith in religion as a source of strength and guidance.

"Many Americans . . . are now cultivating highly personal forms of worship."

Americans Are Turning Away from Organized Religion

Jeremiah Creedon

Although many Americans say they believe in God, they have drastically different conceptions about who or what God is, argues Jeremiah Creedon in the following viewpoint. He asserts that a growing number of Americans are rejecting traditional organized religions such as Christianity and are combining different religions and creating their own belief systems to meet their spiritual needs. As a result, the Untied States is in a state of transition from a predominantly Christian nation to one that is religiously diverse. Although some people have criticized Americans for taking a "cafeteria" approach to religion, Creedon suggests that the increasing amount of religious experimentation and creativity is a positive development. Creedon is a senior editor of the *Utne Reader*, an alternative press publication.

As you read, consider the following questions:
1. What questions are raised by the American trend of private belief systems, according to Creedon?
2. What cultural developments from the 1960s have contributed to America's growing religious diversity, according to the author?
3. What criticisms about New Age beliefs does Creedon record?

Excerpted from "God with a Million Faces," by Jeremiah Creedon, *Utne Reader*, July/August 1998. Reprinted with permission.

A friend of mine I'll call Anne-Marie is the founder of a new religious faith. Like other belief systems throughout the ages, the sect of Anne-Marie exists to address life's most haunting questions. If I ask her why we're born and what happens when we die, her answers suggest that our time on earth has meaning and purpose. Whether I buy it hardly matters. The sect of Anne-Marie has one member, Anne-Marie, and that's plenty.

An artist by trade, Anne-Marie has turned her spirituality into a creative act. Her beliefs are drawn from many sources, some ancient, some new. When Anne-Marie speaks of karma and reincarnation, I hear the influence of Hinduism and Buddhism. Her sense that certain places in nature are sacred is either as new as deep ecology or as old as Shinto. It's hard to say exactly how quantum physics fits into the picture, but she says it does. Beneath it all lies the ethical lexicon of her Christian upbringing, timeworn but still discernible, like the ruins of a Spanish mission.

When I ask her why she left her girlhood church, she's blunt. "I needed beliefs that empower me, and organized religion is disempowering," she says. "It's bogus."

Private Belief Systems

Anne-Marie is one of many Americans who are now cultivating highly personal forms of worship. What observers call "pastiche spirituality" or "religion à la carte" involves combining various beliefs and practices from different sources, or even being a member of two or more distinct religions at the same time. The possible variations are endless—and, as critics warn, so are the chances to lose one's way. Nevertheless, the land now abounds with these private belief systems, each tailored to fit the believer's individual needs.

Sociologists have been following the trend for years; now theologians are beginning to wonder how it will shape religious observance in the future. Does it signal the death of the agrarian-based religions of the ancient Middle East and the birth of new faiths better suited to the modern world? Is a single global belief system emerging, one formed of universal elements gleaned from all the others? Has the growth of individual consciousness reached a point where the old vessels of faith can no longer contain it? Or is it all just a narcissistic reaction among the baby boomers as they approach old age and death?

There are as many answers to these questions as there are new religions. Most observers agree, however, that the trend is real, if not entirely new. Religions, like the peoples and languages that serve as their vehicles, have often clashed and intermingled, and gods have merged, blurred, switched genders, fallen silent, and died, often violently. Even within religions, the gap between official doctrine and actual belief can be immense, despite constant efforts by religious authorities to guard their holy texts from creative misinterpretation.

Cultural Trends

In American history, a "privatized" attitude toward spiritual practice has always been evident, scholars say, but the impulse may now be stronger than ever. The reasons can be traced to powerful cultural forces that have been reshaping modern life since the 1960s.

The rise of feminist consciousness, for instance, has led many to turn a skeptical eye on rituals and texts that smack of male bias. As the feminist writer Carol Lee Flinders has pointed out, many women today "are slow to take in, or take on, the great handed-down monolithic doctrines or credos. We know too much about the strengths of *all* religions, and too much about the weaknesses of these religions as well, particularly where women are concerned." She agrees with feminist historian Gerda Lerner that "disconnection from the sacred seems to be the most fundamentally important way in which women have been disempowered through time." Today, many women are trying to re-establish that connection, either within their faiths or, like Anne-Marie, on their own.

Some say that LSD and the psychedelic subculture played a role in weakening traditional religious ties, giving many a sense of personal mystical union with the divine—along with a heady rhetoric for putting that experience into words. Growing exposure to the world's wisdom traditions has expanded our spiritual vocabulary as well. This exchange has been driven partly by demographic changes that have brought many face-to-face with formerly "exotic" religious beliefs, especially those of Asia. This era may have begun with the Immigration Act of 1965, which eliminated a long-standing bias against Asians and other peoples enforced through quotas based on national origin. The new immigrants included many spiritual teachers whose influence would eventually extend beyond their immediate followers into the popular culture.

The information explosion has been another factor in the rise of do-it-yourself spirituality. Esoteric texts once known to a privileged few now fill the bookstores, their myriad truths laid open to be read and recombined at will. And virtually every work of sacred art, from the caves of Altamira onward, circulates endlessly now, free for the appropriating. This robust spiritual marketplace perfectly suits the consumer mentality that has turned Americans into a nation of comparison shoppers. In an age when we trust ourselves to assemble our own investment portfolios and cancer therapies, why not our religious beliefs?

The insights of modern science may also be pushing many away from traditional faiths. According to science writer Chet Raymo, author of *Skeptics and True Believers*, one of the problems of religion today can be traced to the disconnect between old and new models of the cosmos. "All one has to do is compare the little, earth-centered, egg-shaped cosmos of Shakespeare with a Hubble Deep Field photograph," he says, referring to the countless galaxies now visible through the Hubble Space Telescope. "And yet so much of our traditional religion remains grounded in the old cosmology." The call for a synthesis of science and religion has been heard again and again, but a truly compelling new mythology that's both poetic and scientifically rigorous has yet to appear.

Religious Diversity

The spread of pastiche spirituality is only part of a bigger picture of religious change today. We're living in what observers call an age of extreme "religious pluralism." The same cultural forces that have driven many to leave their inherited faiths have also affected others who have stayed. Almost all the major denominations now contain internal movements that are trying to transform them. Many traditionalists, of course, are fighting to block reforms. Syncretism, the formal term for the blending of rituals and beliefs from different faiths, is a dirty word to conservative worshipers, dreaded like a plague of locusts—and maybe as hard to stop. New hybrid modes of worship are constantly appearing, from the new Christian megachurches, whose mammoth services can resemble arena rock, to tiny garage religions hardly bigger than the average band.

The latest edition of the *Encyclopedia of American Religions* lists more than 2,100 religious groups, a figure that has almost doubled in 20 years. They range from the most straight-laced forms of Judaism and Christianity to UFO cults awaiting deliverance by flying saucer. The influx of Asian religions is clearly mirrored in the *Encyclopedia*, and so is the recent rapid rise of Islam, which other sources put at about 3.5 million adherents. With about 750,000 believers, including 100,000 American converts, Buddhism is said to be the country's fastest-growing faith.

The statistics ultimately yield a portrait full of contradictions. One certainty is that we live in a very religious country—in fact, the United States is generally considered to be the most religious country in the Western industrial world. Though nine out of ten American adults believe that God exists, there's growing disagreement about how God should be described. God is Michelangelo's bearded old man in the Sistine Chapel. God is pure intelligence. God is cosmic energy. God is a Goddess. At least eight out of ten American adults consider themselves to be Christians, but most are hazy about the basic tenets of their faith. The pollsters say that Americans pray more often than they have sex, but no one knows how many consider sex and prayer to be the same thing.

The undeniable reality, concludes George Barna in *The Index of Leading Spiritual Indicators* (Word Publishing, 1996), "is that America is transitioning from a Christian nation to a syncretistic, spiritually diverse society." One result of this spiritual upheaval is a "new perception of religion: a personalized, customized form of faith views which meet personal needs, minimize rules and absolutes, and bear little resemblance to the 'pure' form of any of the world's major religions."

John H. Berthrong, associate dean at Boston University's

School of Theology and director of the Institute for Dialogue Among Religious Traditions, has seen this trend unfold in his classroom. "When I talk to students about their own sense of religious identity, I find that more and more of them have been brought up in homes that are post-Christian," he says. "So to say that they are reacting against Christianity is wrong; they've never been Christians. Even some of the ones who are Christian will say, 'But I really like Taoism and Buddhism too, and my meditation is Vipassana, but I also do a lot of work at my local church because I like the choir.'"

Religions, Cults, and Making Soup

The line between religion and cult, between faith and zealotry, is often difficult to draw. Many religions—Jehovah's Witnesses and Seventh-Day Adventists, for example—were once considered cults. And in the United States, there are as many as 3,500 "new" religious groups. . . . The millennium, disenchantment with organized religion, and the isolation of late 20th-century life have steered religious experimentation in new directions. The New Age [movement] offers a menu of spiritual choices. "What a lot of people will do," says a San Francisco man who combines Hindu mysticism and Tibetan Buddhism in his religious life, "is to take a little from each [New Age theme] and combine them. . . . It's like making soup."

Erica Goode, *U.S. News & World Report*, April 7, 1997.

A Christian theologian and scholar of Confucianism, Berthrong has spent 20 years fostering communication among different religions. His observations on the modern fluidity of belief are the basis of a new book he's writing called *The Divine Deli*. "I think a lot of traditional boundaries for many people are simply dissolving," he says. Berthrong sees a trend toward "multiple citizenship" in a number of separate faiths—and no complete allegiance to any one. In terms of basic issues like child rearing and church fundraising, the trend's potential impact is profound. And that's before anyone raises the touchy matter of doctrine. "Many of the more conservative Christian theologians don't find any of this either amusing or profitable," he adds. "It's one of the areas that really defines the difference between liberal theology and conservative theology.". . .

A Smorgasbord Spirituality

Not everyone thinks that smorgasbord spirituality is a desirable feature of life in the global village, and not all the naysayers are theological conservatives. Many critics take aim at New Age practitioners, who, according to George Barna, share the following characteristics: "faith as a private matter, religious principles from a variety of sources, no centralized religious authority, deity intermingled with self, and more focused upon religious consciousness than religious practice." Barna estimates that roughly 20 percent of American adults are New Agers, at least as he loosely defines them. Many critics dismiss New Agers as spiritual dilettantes who aren't so much seeking the sacred as indulging a hunger for new sensations. Others see traditional religions as works of beauty whose holy texts have been polished over the centuries by many minds; to take an idea from here and there, they argue, is like stealing bricks from ancient temples to build a rickety shrine of one's own.

These reservations are summed up by one of the foremost scholars of comparative religion, Huston Smith, in an interview in *Mother Jones* in December 1997: "What you describe as New Age, and what I call the cafeteria approach to spirituality, is not the way organisms are put together, nor great works of art. And a vital faith is more like an organism or a work of art than it is like a cafeteria tray." Though Smith praises New Agers for their optimism, he also notes their failure to confront the question of "radical evil" or to produce true heroes of compassion like Mother Teresa or the Dalai Lama. At worst, he says, New Age beliefs "can be a kind of private escapism to titillate oneself."

After a lifetime spent studying the world's religions and teaching others to see their underlying unity, Smith, in his late 70s, remains what he has been since birth: a Methodist, despite his gripes about Methodist theology. "I certainly would not choose that messenger if I were starting from scratch," he says, but switching from the faith that formed him is not an acceptable option.

Many younger Americans have fewer qualms about reinventing their religious lives. That's one of the findings reported by Wade Clark Roof, a professor of religion and society at the University of California, Santa Barbara, in *A Generation of Seekers: The Spiritual Journeys of the Baby Boom Generation*, published in 1994. Roof is now working on a sequel, a second look at baby boomers and their beliefs on the verge of the 21st century.

What he has found in his most recent research is a calmer, more group-oriented, but still spiritually restless generation. Many boomers (like Anne-Marie) have assembled private faiths from spiritual bits and pieces, while others have turned to new forms of evangelical Christianity that deliberately appeal to the "seeker mentality." In the mainstream faiths, Roof detects a search for more depth. "People are rediscovering their own traditions, finding there were feminists in the Middle Ages, for instance, or powerful female figures in the Old Testament." As for those who returned to organized religion to give their children a source of moral training, many are dropping out again as the nest empties. "It's still very much a generation whose roots in religion are rather fragile," he says, "and therefore they're still open to exploring. I think that's going to continue throughout their lives."

This approach to faith has deep roots. "Religion historically —and particularly in the American democratic setting—has been one of new combinations, pastiche, the mixing of official themes and folk themes," he says. He notes that strains of transcendentalism, self-help, and positive thinking continue to fuse with evangelical Christianity in curious ways, as in the pop theology of the TV program *Touched by an Angel*. "A lot of the appeal is that this is where many people actually live," Roof notes. "Religion is not just handed down from institutions. Sure, institutions have some power of perpetuation, but individuals take what they hear, reinterpret, recombine, reassemble, and come out in their own lived expressions with styles that are very much tailored to themselves." And that's especially true of people today. What they create has a meaning and coherence that works well for them, he concludes, even if the results may seem less than logically consistent.

At Boston University, John Berthrong sees this same creative capacity for fusing different beliefs in his students. Even when their multiple faiths create contradictions, "they don't worry about it," he says. "It doesn't bother people. You can be a Christian fundamentalist on one level, and a computer programmer working in Houston on space technology, and you'd think somehow that would conflict a bit." But it seldom does, he observes. What Berthrong calls the notion of the organic unity of our minds "doesn't always work quite the way we think it does, especially in religion."

Where is all this religious experimentation headed? Berthrong, the theologian, predicts that existing churches could be in trouble if people cease to identify with a single tradition. Roof, the social scientist, sees a similar pattern of individualized worship developing in Generation X, which suggests the trend is destined to continue into the twenty-first century. Others say we're witnessing the birth of a new consciousness and perhaps a widespread belief system that mirrors it. While this may be a common millennial refrain, not everyone thinks it's realistic, or even desirable. . . .

Religion and Faith

Whatever truth there may be in these projections, the clearest window opened by pastiche spirituality may not be on the future, but into the past. In one sense, an individual's homely, imperfect search for meaning says more about the origins of faith than the polished beauty of a great religious tradition can. An established religion may be a finished work of art, but the personal quest is a creative act, and thus just as authentic in what it says about innate human yearnings and desires. In the quest of Anne-Marie and millions like her, we can see a living example of the primal impulse toward faith, which may be the deepest unity underlying all religions. It's one of the benefits of a tolerant age—that we too, if we choose, can strip away the rich vestments of religious tradition and discover that naked faith is something separate and, ultimately, even more mysterious.

*"A river of animosity toward Christianity
runs through American culture at present."*

Elements of American Society Are Hostile to Religious Believers

Marvin Olasky

Marvin Olasky is a journalism professor at the University of Texas at Austin and a senior fellow at the Acton Institute for the Study of Religion and Liberty. In the following viewpoint, he argues that members of America's cultural and political elite have a negative view toward Christians and Christianity that approaches religious bigotry. While Christians in America do not face life-threatening situations that confront Christians in other parts of the world, Olasky believes they are victimized by mockery and prejudice that does not serve America well. He calls for a national dialogue on anti-Christian bigotry and its consequences.

As you read, consider the following questions:

1. How does Olasky characterize those who disparage Christianity?
2. What three major news stories does the author believe demonstrate evidence of prejudice against Christianity?
3. What comparison does Olasky make between anti-Christian prejudice and racism against blacks?

Excerpted from "Christophobia," by Marvin Olasky, *American Outlook*, Summer 2000. Reprinted with permission.

I am well-acquainted with the Christian Right both from travel and from my own associations as a Christian. But I've also taught at the University of Texas at Austin since 1983, so I have a sense of the intellectual leanings of my liberal-to-radical faculty colleagues and distinctly progressive hometown. These parties typically define Christianity in terms of the sins committed in its name, which is like defining science in terms of those who have rigged experiments or used discoveries to create weapons of mass destruction.

The New Bigotry

This faulty view of Christianity is far from benign. In fact, it has sparked a new wave of religious bigotry in this country, an attitude most intense in New York City and Washington, D.C., as has become clear both to me and to veteran observers such as Michael Horowitz of the Hudson Institute. Many leading American thinkers (some are Jewish, most are secularized liberals from nominally Christian backgrounds) speak of Bible-believing Christians the way earlier establishments spoke about Jews. They vent their scorn in Georgetown salons and at Manhattan dinner parties, and their attitudes are evident in media treatment of religion and America's people of faith.

If this attitude were only a matter of making evangelical Christians uncomfortable, it would be bad but hardly tragic. Words may sting conservative Christians here in America, but sticks and stones break bones of Christians in other parts of the world, such as Indonesia and the Sudan. Standing up as a Bible-believing Christian here may lead to a loss of reputation, but in Saudi Arabia, India, and other countries it can quickly lead to losses of lives. Even so, it is important to note that when Christians are lambasted here, it makes the campaign to protect religious liberty abroad less effective.

Scorn in the salons can also harm the poor within the United States. Even though most of the anti-Christian mockery emanates from the cultural elite, it's still important because the elite's attitude toward Christianity influences whether the nation as a whole decides to embrace the work of faith-based organizations, many of the most effective of which are explicitly evangelical. During the past four years [since 1996], such groups have begun helping women make the transition from welfare to work, and faith-based groups have already proven their effectiveness in helping addicts overcome drug addiction and alcoholism. Faith-based organizations could do much more, but countless federal laws and court rulings stand in their way.

Bigotry Halts Progress

The next president needs to understand how and why important initiatives in many areas have been hindered and sometimes destroyed by what could be called *Christophobia*, the fear of Christianity and the desire to run from it, sometimes into the arms of desperate alternatives. The prevalence and significance of Christophobia become clearer when we look at some of the big news stories of the past two years. During the Clinton impeachment debates of 1998, for example, outright Clinton defenders and forthright Clinton opponents pretty much balanced each other out. [Editor's note: President Bill Clinton was impeached by the House of Representatives in 1998 for legal offenses related to a sexual affair he had with an intern. The impeachment followed an investigation and recommendation by independent prosecutor Kenneth Starr. The Senate tried and acquitted Clinton in 1999.] The crucial role thus fell to what we might call the nonjudgmental centrists. They didn't like Clinton, but they hated and feared special prosecutor Kenneth Starr, the embodiment, to them, of contemporary American Christianity.

Starr's moral clarity was a constant indictment of the ethical sloth of the many Americans who refused to look hard at the facts and bring justice to a wrongdoer. (This pattern was similar to the way that the presence of a happy adopted child works as an indictment of those who favor abortion.) The nonjudgers didn't want to take a stand, but they wanted to feel perfectly upright, and they were angry that Starr would not let them. Antipathy to Christianity, magnified by the common press depiction of Starr as the embodiment of a narrow fundamentalism, killed the impeachment drive and left many legislators clinging to censure proposals with little constitutional footing.

Another visible manifestation of Christophobia occurred

in April 1999 after the Columbine High School shootings, when Americans once again had to focus on the holes in our souls. [In an armed attack that stunned the nation, 12 students and one teacher at a Colorado high school were shot and killed by two schoolmates who subsequently killed themselves.] *Wall Street Journal* columnist Peggy Noonan observed that "a gun and a Bible have a few things in common. Both are small, black, have an immediate heft, and are dangerous—the first to life, the second to the culture of death." Noonan also wrote, "A man called into Christian radio this morning and said a true thing. He said, 'Those kids were sick and sad, and if a teacher had talked to one of them and said, "Listen, there's a way out, there really is love out there that will never stop loving you, there's a real God, and I want to be able to talk to you about Him"; if that teacher had intervened that way, he would have been hauled into court.'"

Reprinted by permission of Chuck Asay and Creators Syndicate.

Noonan's column generated some very revealing letters, such as the following one which appeared the very next day in the *Wall Street Journal*: "I profoundly wish Peggy Noonan were right, [but] have we forgotten Jim Jones of Jonestown, who convinced parents that it was God's will to put cyanide into their children's Kool-Aid? Or the killing in the Balkans, where weapons are being blessed by priests?" Such cynicism has become commonplace: mention anything positive done in the name of the God of the Bible, and someone will immediately mention something negative. Although politicians tend to indicate loose allegiance to the concept that faith in God is part of the solution to the nation's innumerable social ills, many really consider it part of the problem. This entrenched antagonism has elevated psychiatrists to the level of priests, and we parade them in when mass shootings occur, pretending that is enough while resolutely refusing to do things that will give kids real hope. This is happening because so many Americans are searching for a way out, a way of feeling moral without having to answer to any power higher than themselves, and in particular to respond to the claims of Christ.

Antipathy Toward Christians

A third major example of antipathy toward Christians occurred during the early months of 2000, when John McCain entered the media spotlight. [The Arizona senator was then competing for the 2000 Republican presidential nomination with Texas governor and eventual nominee George W. Bush.] By March 1, neither John McCain nor George W. Bush was running the campaign he had planned to execute. Bush, after planning to run as a moderate conservative, was being excoriated as a captive of the Christian Right. The McCain campaign changed even more remarkably. According to reporter Richard Sisk, "McCain said his candidacy has undergone a transformation," and that he had become "determined to rid the GOP of big money and the Christian Right influence." This was sensational because the Christian Right was a large source of the GOP's volunteers and was probably the Republican Party's moral center as well. Although McCain and his followers claimed no animus toward Christianity in general, their rhetoric was similar to that displayed by Christophobes concerning Ken Starr and the need for a religious revival at Columbine High. . . .

In short, the most dramatic news stories of the past three

years—impeachment, Columbine, McCain—all concluded as they did because a river of animosity toward Christianity runs through American culture at present. The need for change is evident, but many journalistic and academic leaders oppose a broad turn toward Christianity, even though this religion has been the paramount agent of positive change in Western culture throughout the centuries, despite the sins of individual believers. . . .

A New Discussion

Washington journalists tend to overestimate the clout and underestimate the intelligence of Christian conservatives, and they are prone to envision vast Right-wing conspiracies bubbling out of the hinterlands. Anyone who points out American Christians' distinct lack of power relative to the cultural authority of secular liberalism is immediately branded a whiner and complainer and probably a conspirator. The next president can start correcting this cultural imbalance by proposing that it is at least proper to begin talking about this problem. Right now, for example, it is politically incorrect to talk about black racism, which some say (on the supposition that blacks don't have the power to be racist) cannot exist. Similarly, many Washington and New York journalists believe that Christians generally are in charge in America and thus cannot suffer discrimination.

President Clinton engendered a national discussion of racism, but it lost steam because there was nothing much left to talk about: no major political leader backs it, and no significant presidential candidate in recent years has claimed that any black leaders personify evil. Jews, who historically have been on the receiving end of much religious bigotry, are largely free from public bigotry of the sort now directed toward Christians. That a leading presidential candidate— and one with enormous press support—was able to express open hostility toward conservative Christians tells us that the next president should initiate a national dialogue on anti-Christian bigotry and its consequences in both domestic and international policy.

"Disbelief in God must become as legitimate as belief in God in every forum of American life."

American Society Is Hostile to Religious Nonbelievers

Alan M. Dershowitz

Alan M. Dershowitz is a law professor at Harvard Law School and a prolific author whose books include *The Genesis of Justice: 10 Stories of Biblical Injustice That Led to the 10 Commandments* and *The Vanishing American Jew: In Search of Jewish Identity for the Next Century*. In the following viewpoint, he contends that millions of Americans who are religious skeptics or nonbelievers are afraid to make their views known for fear of being considered immoral and unfit for public office. The result is that religious nonbelievers who openly express their views are accorded a second-class status, something that Dershowitz contends is unfair and that goes against the American ideal of religious freedom.

As you read, consider the following questions:
1. How is Europe different from the United States in religious belief and expression, according to Dershowitz?
2. What does the author call for religious skeptics to do?
3. How have religious views changed over the past thousand years, according to Dershowitz?

Reprinted, with permission, from "Taking Disbelief Out of the Closet," by Alan M. Dershowitz, *Free Inquiry*, Summer 1999.

The most insidious genre of censorial political correctness in America today involves belief in God. Few people in public life are prepared to disclose that they are atheists, agnostics, skeptics, or humanists. For a politician, such a declaration would be death as evidenced by a recent controversy in Canada when a young rising star in Parliament introduced a resolution seeking to remove a phrase from Canada's Charter of Rights and Freedoms that declared "the supremacy of God." He was immediately punished by parliamentary leaders and forced to apologize. Although there are many closet disbelievers in politics today, few have the courage to acknowledge their skepticism in the face of religious hegemony.

Even academics, whose tenure guarantees them the right to speak freely without consequence, rarely publicize their disbelief for fear of alienating students, alumni, and the administration. *Being* an atheist or agnostic in America is relatively cost free, so long as you remain in the closet. Most public institutions have a "Don't ask, don't tell" policy when it comes to disbelief.

The situation is very different throughout Europe, where atheism and agnosticism are openly acknowledged. Numerous heads of government have made no secret of their disbelief. Despite—perhaps because of—the fact that most European nations have established churches, there is more actual freedom of disbelief in Europe than there is in the United States, whose Constitution guarantees freedom of and from religion. Established churches have a way of encouraging free thinking among those who don't want to be told what they may believe or disbelieve.

Religious Hegemony

The time has come for atheists, agnostics, skeptics, and humanists to come out of the closet and to openly confront the religious hegemony in America that has created a political correctness so powerful that even the most courageous are afraid to violate it openly. Unless such a challenge is mounted, the situation will simply grow more dangerous. Already the Democratic Party, which traditionally was more secular than the Republican, has begun to run on God's coattails. It started with Jimmy Carter. It got worse with Bill Clinton. And it promises to get even worse with Al Gore, who is explicitly pandering to what he calls "faith-based organizations." More and more American politicians are publicly advertising their religious beliefs—that they have been saved, that they have been reborn, and that they have accepted Jesus as their personal Savior. This puts additional pressure on other politicians to match and exceed their rivals in public devotion to God. Some lobbying groups rank candidates by the fervor of their religious commitments.

A Repressed Minority

As the last repressed minority in America, religious dissenters need to stand up and be counted. We need to wage a campaign to defend our rights. And we need to persuade our fellow citizens that equal protection of the laws should apply to all citizens, believers and unbelievers alike.

There are millions of Americans who do not profess a belief in God. We are a significant minority. Yet our voice is all too rarely heard in the public square. Intolerant attitudes and prejudice against us continue to fester. Heretics and iconoclasts are often considered the pariahs of society.

Paul Kurtz, *Free Inquiry*, Summer 2000.

One reason why so many disbelievers are unwilling to acknowledge their views with intellectual honesty is that the religious establishment has managed to persuade large segments of the American public that there is some correlation between belief in a supernatural God and human ethics and morals. Disbelievers are deemed immoral. Consider the response of Canadian Parliamentarian Randy White to the Parliamentarian who tried to remove God from the Charter: "What do we stand for in this country? What are the values? What are the morals? Every time you turn around, you see government slipping lower and lower into the gutters of this country." But history has shown that if there is any correlation between belief in God and personal morality—which I personally reject—it is as likely to be a negative as a positive one. Surely as much immorality has been committed in the name of religion as any other cause. The millions murdered by cynical, godless tyrants such as Hitler and Stalin are dwarfed by those killed in the names of Jesus, Muhammad, and Jehovah throughout history. In any event, Stalin and Hitler do not represent the morality of disbelievers any more than Torquemada represents the views of believers.

The most moral people in the world are those who act self-lessly without promise of reward or threat of punishment in the hereafter. French philosopher Blaise Pascal's wager—that it is better to bet on the existence of God even if He doesn't exist, than to risk the punishment of disbelieving—is nothing more than a crude cost-benefit calculus having little to do with morality. I am aware of no empirical data showing that believers are less likely to commit crimes, cheat on their wives, or abuse their children than nonbelievers. Our prisons are full of people who profess religious beliefs, and the most benef-icent human beings include many who are disbelievers.

A Call for Openness

I suspect that tens of millions of Americans are skeptics or nonbelievers but are afraid to speak out. We must make it safe for such people to express their views openly. Disbelief in God must become as legitimate as belief in God in every forum of American life. We must confront religious authoritarianism in the marketplace of ideas, with respect but with vigor.

Having called for more openness in the expression of views regarding the existence of God, let me follow my own example. I am a skeptic about everything, including God and atheism. I am not certain about issues of cosmology. Some-times I believe that our universe is the result of random forces. Other times I believe that there must be some order or purpose, though I do not begin to understand what or who it could be. I do not expect that these cosmic doubts will ever be resolved in my mind. I am more certain that the miraculous stories that form the basis of most religious be-liefs are myths. Yet I respect the Bible and enjoy reading and teaching it. Indeed, I find it even more fascinating as a hu-man creation than as a divine revelation. I consider myself a committed Jew, but I do not believe that being a Jew re-quires belief in the supernatural. When I attend synagogue, as I often do, or conduct Sabbath, Passover, or Chanukah services at home, I recite prayers. I am comfortable with these apparent contradictions. I am part of a long tradition that links to my heritage through the words and melodies of prayer. Indeed, it is while praying that I experience my greatest doubts about God, and it is while looking at the stars that I make the leap of faith. But it is not faith in the empirical truths of religious stories or in the authority of hierarchical religious organizations. If there is a governing force, He (or She or It) is certainly not in touch with those who purport to be speaking on His behalf.

The important point is that everyone must have the right to question faith and to decide these eternal issues by their own lights, without being condemned if they disagree with today's religious consensus. Remember that religious views change over the millennium. People were killed for believing in Jesus and then for not believing in Jesus, for accepting Catholicism and for rejecting Catholicism, and for many other religious disagreements. Today, thankfully, Americans are not killed for their religious beliefs or disbeliefs. But they are condemned as immoral and unfit for public office if they publicly declare their skepticism. The world must be made safe and secure for disbelievers. America was founded on religious dissent and skepticism. We must not accept religious hegemony or preference for religion in public life. Atheists and agnostics are every bit as American, every bit as moral and every bit as qualified to hold public office as people who believe in an intervening God. Disbelievers should not accept second-class status in a nation whose traditions and laws forbid tests of faith as a condition of citizenship or office holding.

Periodical Bibliography

The following articles have been selected to supplement the diverse views presented in this chapter. Addresses are provided for periodicals not indexed in the *Readers' Guide to Periodical Literature*, the *Alternative Press Index*, the *Social Sciences Index*, or the *Index to Legal Periodicals and Books*.

Peter Beinart	"Visions 21/How Will We Live: Will Politicians Matter? Religion Will Increasingly Replace Electoral Politics as the Realms Where Battles for the National Soul Are Fought," *Time*, February 21, 2000.
Jonah Blank	"The Muslim Mainstream," *U.S. News & World Report*, July 20, 1998.
M. Stanton Evans	"Reexamining the Religious Roots of Freedom," *USA Today*, September 1995.
John Garvey	"Opting Out of Belief," *Commonweal*, May 19, 2000.
Gary Glenn and John Stack	"America: Fundamentally Religious," *World & I*, December 1999. Available from 3600 New York Ave. NE, Washington, DC 20002.
Jane Lampman	"Faith Returns to the Public Square," *Christian Science Monitor*, June 29, 2000.
Jack Miles	"Religion Makes a Comeback. (Belief to Follow)," *New York Times Magazine*, December 7, 1997.
Jan Nattier	"American Buddhists: Who Are They?" *Current*, September 1997.
Richard N. Ostling	"America's Ever-Changing Religious Landscape," *Brookings Review*, Spring 1999.
Daniel Pipes	"In Muslim America," *National Review*, February 21, 2000.
Roger Scruton	"Bibles and Broomsticks," *National Review*, September 27, 1999.
Edward S. Shapiro	"American Jews and the Problem of Identity," *Society*, September/October 1997.
Margaret Talbot	"Inward Christian Soldiers," *New York Times Magazine*, February 27, 2000.
John Updike	"The Future of Faith," *New Yorker*, November 29, 1999.
David Van Biema	"Buddhism in America," *Time*, October 13, 1997.

Can Religion Solve America's Social Problems?

Chapter Preface

Religious groups and organizations have long been involved in charity and social reform efforts. In recent years a growing number of political and social leaders in the United States have turned toward religious or "faith-based" organizations to assist or even take over the administration of social welfare functions previously handled by government, including welfare benefits, prisons, and drug and alcohol treatment. Proponents of such programs argue that they can achieve superior results because of the special commitment religion can inspire in both social welfare providers and recipients.

In 1996 Congress passed welfare reform legislation dubbed "Charitable Choice" that permitted religious groups who assisted and counseled welfare recipients (and who made their religious message an integral part of their work) to receive government funding. Al Gore and George W. Bush, the major nominees for the 2000 presidential election, both endorsed Charitable Choice and argued for its expansion to other religious groups who worked with the homeless or with troubled youth. However, the use of religious organizations to tackle various social problems raises two large questions. One is whether religious groups can actually supplant the welfare work now done by the government. The other is whether such programs, especially those with government funding, blur the constitutional separation of church and state that many argue should remain a fundamental principle in American society. The viewpoints in this chapter examine these and other questions concerning religion's role in solving America's social problems.

| "Religious practice appears to have enormous potential for addressing today's social problems."

Religion Can Solve America's Social Problems

Patrick F. Fagan

Patrick F. Fagan is a research fellow at the Heritage Foundation, a conservative Washington, D.C.-based think tank. He previously worked in the federal Department of Health and Human Services and as a family therapist and sociologist. In the following viewpoint, he argues that the practice of religion in the United States is both an individual and social good that has numerous positive effects in countering social problems such as family breakdown, substance abuse, and welfare dependency. People who practice religion, Fagan claims, are more likely to have strong families, to have higher self-esteem, and to be good citizens. He concludes that makers of public policy should acknowledge the beneficial aspects of religion.

As you read, consider the following questions:
1. What is the relationship between religion and mental health, according to Fagan?
2. What distinction does the author make between "intrinsic" and "extrinsic" forms of religion?
3. What policy implications does Fagan draw from his study of the effects of religion?

Excerpted from "Why Religion Matters: The Impact of Religious Practice on Social Stability," by Patrick F. Fagan, *The Heritage Foundation Backgrounder*, no.1064, January 25, 1996. Reprinted with permission.

When policymakers consider America's grave social problems, including violent crime and rising illegitimacy, substance abuse, and welfare dependency, they should heed the findings in the professional literature of the social sciences on the positive consequences that flow from the practice of religion.

For example, there is ample evidence that:

- The strength of the family unit is intertwined with the practice of religion. Churchgoers are more likely to be married, less likely to be divorced or single, and more likely to manifest high levels of satisfaction in marriage.
- Church attendance is the most important predictor of marital stability and happiness.
- The regular practice of religion helps poor persons move out of poverty. Regular church attendance, for example, is particularly instrumental in helping young people to escape the poverty of inner-city life.
- Religious belief and practice contribute substantially to the formation of personal moral criteria and sound moral judgment.
- Regular religious practice generally inoculates individuals against a host of social problems, including suicide, drug abuse, out-of-wedlock births, crime, and divorce.
- The regular practice of religion also encourages such beneficial effects on mental health as less depression (a modern epidemic), more self-esteem, and greater family and marital happiness.
- In repairing damage caused by alcoholism, drug addiction, and marital breakdown, religious belief and practice are a major source of strength and recovery.
- Regular practice of religion is good for personal physical health: It increases longevity, improves one's chances of recovery from illness, and lessens the incidence of many killer diseases. . . .

Religious practice appears to have enormous potential for addressing today's social problems. . . .

Religion and Social Breakdown

The practice of religion has beneficial effects on behavior and social relations: on illegitimacy, crime and delinquency, welfare dependency, alcohol and drug abuse, suicide, depression, and general self-esteem.

Illegitimacy. One of the most powerful of all factors in preventing out-of-wedlock births is the regular practice of religious belief. Given the growing crisis in out-of-wedlock births, their effects, and the huge social and economic costs to national and state budgets, this should be of major interest to policymakers.

It has long been known that intensity of religious practice is closely related to adolescent virginity and sexual restraint and control. . . . Reviews of the literature demonstrate that, nearly without exception, religious practice sharply reduces the incidence of premarital intercourse. The reverse is also true: The absence of religious practice accompanies sexual permissiveness and premarital sex. This is confirmed in numerous studies, including a 1991 analysis of the federal government's National Longitudinal Survey of Youth. . . .

The religious practices of parents, particularly their unity on religious issues, powerfully influence the behavior of children. Thus, for policymakers interested in reducing teenage (and older) out-of-wedlock births, the lesson is clear: Religious belief and regular worship reduce the likelihood of this form of family breakdown. . . .

Crime and Delinquency. A review of the small amount of research done on the relationship between crime and religion shows that states with more religious populations tend to have fewer homicides and fewer suicides.

A four-year longitudinal, stratified, random-sample study of high school students in the Rocky Mountain region, published in 1975, demonstrated that religious involvement significantly decreased drug use, delinquency, and premarital sex, and also increased self-control. A 1989 study of midwestern high school students replicated these findings. Similarly, young religious adults in Canada were found in a 1979 study to be less likely to use or sell narcotics, to gamble, or to destroy property.

What is true for youth is also true for adults. Religious behavior, as opposed to mere attitude or affiliation, is associated with reduced crime. . . .

In research conducted in the late 1980s—controlling for

family, economic, and religious backgrounds—a research team from the University of Nevada found that black men who eventually ended up in prison and those who did not came respectively from two different groups: those who did not go to church, or stopped going around ten years of age, and those who went regularly. This failure of faith at the onset of adolescence parallels the pattern found among those who become alcoholics or drug addicts. Clearly, the family's inability to inspire regular religious worship among emerging young adults is a sign of internal weakness.

Welfare Dependency. In his classic study *The Protestant Ethic and the Spirit of Capitalism*, Max Weber, the preeminent German sociologist . . . demonstrated the connection between religious practice and financial well-being among Protestants. Other work on the same theme shows that this is not confined to Protestants, but that it applies across a longer period of history and across denominational lines.

Religion and Prosperity

This link between religion and prosperity has important implications for the poor. In 1985, for instance, Richard B. Freeman of the National Bureau of Economic Research reported that:

> [Church attendance] is associated with substantial differences in the behavior of [black male youths from poverty-stricken inner-city neighborhoods] and thus in their chances to "escape" from inner city poverty. It affects allocation of time, school-going, work activity and the frequency of socially deviant activity. . . . It is important to recognize that our analysis has identified an important set of variables that separate successful from unsuccessful young persons in the inner city. There is a significant number of inner city youth, readily identifiable, who succeed in escaping that pathology of inner-city slum life.

Ongoing studies by Professor Ranald Jarrell of the Department of Education at Arizona State University West show the power of religious belief and practice in encouraging a spirit of optimism among socially at-risk but advancing children. . . .

Data from the National Longitudinal Survey of Youth (NLSY), the best national sample for tracking the development of America's youth from the late 1970s, clearly indicate the difference regular religious practice makes for those who grew up in poverty in the 1970s and 1980s. Among those who attended church weekly in both 1979 and 1982, average family income in 1993 was $37,021; among those who never attended church in 1979 or 1982, however, average family income in 1993 was $24,361—a difference of $12,660. . . .

Substance Abuse

Alcohol and Drug Abuse. The relationship between religious practice and the moderate use or avoidance of alcohol is well documented, regardless of whether denominational beliefs prohibit the use of alcohol. According to general studies, the higher the level of religious involvement, the less likely the use or abuse of alcohol.

Persons who abuse alcohol rarely have a strong religious commitment. In their study of the development of alcohol abuse, David Larson and William P. Wilson, professors of psychiatry at Northwestern University School of Medicine, found that nine out of ten alcoholics had lost interest in religion in their teenage years, in sharp contrast to teenagers generally, among whom interest in religion increased by almost 50 percent and declined by only 14 percent. Robert Coombs and his colleagues at the University of California at Los Angeles School of Medicine found that alcohol abuse is 300 percent higher among those who do not attend church.

Drug and alcohol use is lowest in the most conservative religious denominations and highest in non-religious groups, while liberal church groups have use rates just slightly lower than those for non-religious groups. But for all groups, religious commitment correlates with absence of drug abuse. . . .

Alcoholics Anonymous, the major organization combating alcoholism in America, has known for over half a century that the most effective element in its program is its religious or spiritual component. David Larson of the National Institute for Healthcare Research notes: "Even after alcoholism has been established, religion is often a powerful force in achieving abstinence. Alcoholics Anonymous (AA) uses religion, invoking a Higher Power to help alcoholics recover from addiction."

The Work of Progressive Religious Groups

Contrary to what many may think, religion is alive and well in America—and a good deal of what it says and does is strikingly progressive. . . .

In Los Angeles, you'll find the progressive religious tradition alive in Clergy and Laity United for Economic Justice (CLUE), a coalition of ministers, priests, and rabbis that proved decisive in getting the city's landmark living-wage ordinance passed in 1997. . . .

You'll find that same sort of dynamism in the Greater Boston Interfaith Organization (GBIO). At its founding meeting in 1999, nearly 5,000 people heard inner-city black Pentecostal ministers, suburban Unitarian and Episcopalian clergy, a rabbi, an imam, and Boston's Archbishop Bernard Cardinal Law, all preaching a new era of multiracial, multi-ethnic, faith-led urban renewal. Nearly 100 congregations, union locals, and community groups have now begun working together to improve low-income housing, city schools, and job conditions for new immigrants. . . .

Over in East Brooklyn, a number of mostly black and Hispanic activist ministers and laypeople working together as the Nehemiah Project have raised millions in loans from their local churches and national denominations to build or rehabilitate nearly 5,000 units of low-income housing over the past 15 years. The group's success is now being copied by new Nehemiah Projects in other cities around the country.

Richard Parker, *The American Prospect*, January 17, 2000.

Paralleling the research on alcohol addiction, an early [1976] review of studies of drug addiction found a lack of religious commitment to be a predictor of who abuses drugs. Many more recent studies replicate this finding. . . . According to Jerald G. Bachman of the Institute for Social Research at the University of Michigan, "Factors we found to be most important in predicting use of marijuana and other drugs during the late 1970's remained most important during the early 1980's. Drug use is below average among those with strong religious commitments." The more powerfully addictive the drug being considered, the more powerful is the impact of church attendance in preventing its use. . . .

Louis A. Cancellaro of the Department of Psychiatry at the Veterans Administration in Johnson City, Tennessee, writes that, "Like their fathers, addicts are less religiously involved than their normal peers, and during adolescence, less frequently make decisions either to become more interested in religion or to commit themselves to a religious philosophy to live by."

In reviewing the religious treatment of addicts, research psychiatrists at the Duke University Department of Psychiatry concluded in 1992: "[The] role of religious commitment and religiously oriented treatment programs can be significant factors which ought to be considered and included when planning a mix of appropriate treatment alternatives. . . . Perhaps the greatest advantage of religious programs is their recourse to churches as a support system. . . . Religious treatment programs are not suitable for everyone. For those men and women who can accept the creeds, rituals, and commitments required of such programs there seem to be certain advantages."

Religion and Mental Health

Suicide. The practice of religion reduces the rate of suicide, both in the United States and abroad. In fact, the rate of church attendance predicts the suicide rate better than any other factor (including unemployment, traditionally regarded as the most powerful variable). Those who attend church frequently are four times less likely to commit suicide than those who never attend. Conversely, the national decline in church attendance is associated with a heightened suicide rate; fluctuations in church attendance rates in the 1970s paralleled the suicide rates for different subgroups: whites, blacks, men, and women. . . .

Depression. Religion appears to reduce the incidence of depression among those with medical problems. For instance, University of Michigan Professor of Sociology David Williams conducted a randomized survey of 720 adults suffering from leg and hip injuries in New Haven, Connecticut, in 1990. Those who attended religious services regularly were less depressed and less distressed by life events than those who did not. This finding held across age, race, socioeconomic status, educational attainment, and religious affiliation. Religious affiliation alone did not have these effects, but religious behavior did.

Younger people also tend to experience fewer of the anxieties of growing up if they are religious. For instance, both male and female Texas high-schoolers found that religious beliefs gave meaning to their lives and reduced the incidence of depression among them.

Self-esteem. The absence of self-esteem weakens the personality and puts the person at greater risk for crime, addictions, and other social maladies. In all religious denominations, psychological weaknesses decrease as religious orthodoxy increases. Among college students, for instance, the practice of religion was shown in 1969 to have a positive effect on mental health; students involved with campus ministries were much healthier and made much less use of mental health services.

Significantly, self-esteem is linked to a person's image of God. Those with high self-esteem think of God primarily as loving, while those with low self-esteem think of God primarily as punitive. This was observed by Carl Jung, one of the most influential pioneers of modern psychology and psychotherapy: "Among all my patients in the second half of my life . . . there has not been one whose problem in the last resort was not that of finding a religious outlook on life. It is safe to say that every one of them fell ill because he had lost that which the living religions of every age have given their followers and none of them has been really healed who did not regain his religious outlook.". . .

"Intrinsic" and "Extrinsic" Religious Behavior

Recent advances in the investigation of religious behavior have led social scientists to distinguish between two distinct categories or orientations: "intrinsic" and "extrinsic." Intrinsic practice is God-oriented and based on beliefs which transcend the person's own existence. Research shows this form of religious practice to be beneficial. Extrinsic practice is self-oriented and characterized by outward observance, not internalized as a guide to behavior or attitudes. The evidence suggests this form of religious practice is actually more harmful than no religion: Religion directed toward some end other than God, or the transcendent, typically degenerates into a rationalization for the pursuit of other ends such as status, personal security, self justification, or sociability.

The difference between these two forms of religious practice have implications for future research and for the interpretation of all research on religious practice. There is a radical difference between what religious people know to be conversion of the spirit or heart and simply conforming external behavior for its own sake, or for benefits derived from religious behavior. . . .

The two orientations lead to two very different sets of psychological effects. For instance, "intrinsics" have a greater sense of responsibility and greater internal control, are more self-motivated, and do better in their studies. By contrast, "extrinsics" are more likely to be dogmatic, authoritarian, and less responsible, to have less internal control, to be less self-directed, and to do less well in their studies. Intrinsics are more concerned with moral standards, conscientiousness, discipline, responsibility, and consistency than are extrinsically religious people. They also are more sensitive to others and more open to their own emotions. By contrast, extrinsics are more self-indulgent, indolent, and likely to lack dependability. For example, the most racially prejudiced people turn out to be those who go to church occasionally and those who are extrinsic in their practice of religion. . . .

From a purely social science standpoint, the intrinsic form of religion is thus good and desirable, and the extrinsic form is harmful. Religious teachers, without being utilitarian, would agree. . . .

Policy Implications

The evidence indicates strongly that it is a good social policy to foster the widespread practice of religion. It is bad social policy to block it. The widespread practice of religious beliefs is one of America's greatest national resources. It strengthens individuals, families, communities, and society as a whole. It significantly affects educational and job attainment and reduces the incidence of such major social problems as out-of-wedlock births, drug and alcohol addiction, crime, and delinquency. No other dimension of the nation's life, other than the health of the family (which the data show also is tied powerfully to religious practice) should be of more concern to those who guide the future course of the United States. . . .

America needs a major national debate on the true role of religion in a free and pluralistic society. For many decades, the once-prominent place of religion in society has been eroded. Religious leaders, who should be in the forefront of moral and spiritual renewal, have been cowed into a strange timidity. Americans of religious belief should not be bullied into believing that in all things related to the public good, religion is to remain off limits. The constitutional freedom of religion does not mean the constitutional barring of religion from the public square. . . .

The available evidence clearly demonstrates that regular religious practice is both an individual and social good. It is a powerful answer to many of our most significant social problems, some of which, including out-of-wedlock births, have reached catastrophic proportions. Furthermore, it is available to all, and at no cost. . . .

Many of the goals of social policy and social work can be attained, indirectly and powerfully, through the practice of religion. None of this invalidates education or social work, which operate at a different level of the human condition. However, as demands for social work outstrip (and give every indication of far outstripping) social work resources, it is good to know that the practice of religion is a powerful ally.

The practice of religion is good for individuals, families, states, and the nation. It improves health, learning, economic well-being, self-control, self-esteem, and empathy. It reduces the incidence of social pathologies, such as out-of-wedlock births, crime, delinquency, drug and alcohol addiction, health problems, anxieties, and prejudices.

The Founding Fathers, in their passionate love of freedom, promoted the freedom of all Americans to practice their religious beliefs, but Congress and the courts have crowded religion out of the public square. It is time to bring it back. Religious practice can and should be factored into the planning and debate on the nation's urgent social problems. Americans cannot build their future without drawing on the strengths that come to them from the practice of their religious beliefs.

> "Considering the persistence of religious bigotry, not to mention the history of religious warfare, it is a bit perverse to promote religion as an antidote for social disorder."

Religion May Not Solve America's Social Problems

Wendy Kaminer

Wendy Kaminer, a lawyer and social critic, is a fellow at Radcliffe College and the author of several books, including *True Love Waits: Essays and Criticism*. In the following viewpoint, she argues that although many people believe that religion can be uniquely effective in dealing with crime, drug abuse and other social problems, there is little evidence that organized religion has positive social benefits or moralizing effects. Religious belief can result in cruelty and bigotry. Kaminer defends atheism from charges that it leads to immorality and asserts that atheists can be as virtuous and socially responsible as religious people.

As you read, consider the following questions:
1. Why is it difficult to make generalizations about religious belief as a predictor of good or bad behavior, according to Kaminer?
2. What advantages do atheists have in forming moral character, according to the author?
3. What examples of religious cruelty does Kaminer describe?

Reprinted, with permission, from "Atheists Can Be Moral,Too," by Wendy Kaminer, IntellectualCapital.com, December 11, 1997.

Considering the dismal state of science education, there are probably more Americans who believe in God than the law of gravity. It is an article of faith among these believers (some 95% of the population) that religion is essential to virtue. So . . . it is not surprising to find faith being touted as the solution to drug abuse, teenage pregnancy and other social ills.

Some churches do oppose government funding of faith-based social services: the Presbyterian Church USA, the American Baptist Churches USA and the United Methodist Church were part of a coalition that fought federal legislation giving churches a right to administer federally-funded welfare programs. But politicians oppose church-state partnerships at their peril, and it is virtually impossible to imagine any candidate for public office questioning the ameliorative effect of religion—although there is little empirical proof of it.

Realities of Religious Belief

People accept with faith the value of religious belief. I suppose they must. It is probably impossible to measure the historic effect of organized religion on human welfare. How do you balance the Inquisition with the Civil Rights Movement, for instance?

It is equally difficult to make generalizations about the character of believers or to use religious belief as a predictor of virtuous behavior. Religious people practiced and opposed slavery, after all. What can we infer from this—that, as novelist Mary McCarthy wrote, "Religion is only good for good people"?

McCarthy's dismissal of religion's moralizing effect probably would not evoke much agreement today, although many believers would be comfortable with the converse notion that religion is only bad for bad people. Even that principle, however, is not applied consistently. That is why political and religious biases are likely to determine whether we attribute acts of terrorism to individual terrorists or the religions that breed them. Americans may blame Moslem fundamentalism for the acts of Iranian terrorists a little more readily than they will blame Orthodox Judaism for the assassination of [Israeli prime minister] Yitzhak Rabin or the

massacre of Palestinians at a West Bank mosque by Orthodox extremists. Absent particular religious or ethnic prejudice, religious belief generally gets the benefit of a doubt. It
is credited for the good that people do and excused for the
evils that it encourages.

Atheism and the Golden Rule

Atheism, however, is identified with evil and moral anarchy,
and some atheists indeed are less than virtuous—just like
some religious people. As a group, disbelievers surely are no
better than believers, but are they worse?

It is difficult to mount an affirmative defense of atheism
without sounding as self-righteous as religious zealots quot-
ing scripture. But you can, at least, acknowledge what atheism is not: It is not inherently nihilistic, as many believe; it
does not deprive you of moral standards or instincts.

The Evils of Religion

Though accused of demonic deeds and in most circles ostra-
cized, I still believe that theism should be publicly challenged.
Besides being intellectually dubious, it begets organized religion, whose moral history scarcely inspires confidence. While
institutionalized religion performs some valuable functions, it
has an enormous capacity for ill. As Steven Weinberg, Nobel
laureate in physics, recently noted in a speech to the members
of the American Association for the Advancement of Science:
"With or without it, you'd have good people doing good
things and evil people doing evil things. But for good people
to do evil things, it takes religion."

Gary Sloan, *Free Inquiry*, Summer 2000.

Except for the sadomasochistic among us, childhood
lessons in the Golden Rule may serve as well as fables about
God handing Moses a tablet of commandments in establishing acceptable behavior. (In fact, sadomasochists are apt to
feel more at home with religion given its occasional habits of
authoritarianism and self-flagellation.) Nor does atheism encourage hedonism. The conviction that there is no cosmic
justice can fuel a commitment to the cause of earthly justice.
Atheism denies you the luxury of believing that the wrongs
of this world will be avenged in the next.

Atheists are not magical thinkers; without faith, people celebrate reason, an underrated quality. . . . This does not mean that they disdain emotionalism, like [novelist Charles] Dickens' Mr. Gradgrind, in the belief that human beings are like computers. Passion is hardly dependent on a belief in the supernatural. Atheists are apt to be as irrational in their preferences and personal lives as believers, but they are probably less likely to consult their horoscopes or suppose they have been abducted by aliens.

They are as likely, however, to be guided by sentiment, or instinct, in addition to reason. To answer moral questions, questions about ends and not means, a non-believer will consult "his own heart," [philosopher] Bertrand Russell observed. These questions "belong to a realm . . . of emotion and feeling and desire . . . a realm which is not that of reason though it should be in no degree contrary to it." Faithlessness can make moral choices harder; it demands an active inner life as well as a capacity for empathy and engagement with the world.

Besides, science can explain our ethical impulses as well as religion. In *Descartes' Error*, an intriguing study of the relationship between emotion, reasoning and moral judgment, neurologist Antonio Damasio suggests that there are "biological mechanisms behind the most sublime human behavior." (You will be guided by these mechanisms whether or not you believe that God designed them.)

Common sense tells us that parental nurture, as well as a vision of the divine, helps make people good. It is possible, after all, to instill respect for justice and generally accepted notions of ethical behavior in children without encouraging them to believe in God. (I grew up in a secular home and have not committed any sins much worse than blasphemy yet.) Acknowledging that there are no gods on their side, it may be easier to imbue them with moral modesty and respect for differing worldviews.

The Divisiveness of Religion

Faithlessness also can avoid the cruel sectarianism often engendered by faith. In Alabama, where a judge has posted a copy of the Ten Commandments in his courtroom in defiance of federal law, Jewish children are forced to participate in

Christian religious observances in the Pike County public schools. Organized, official religious activities are not uncommon in the nation's schools, especially in the South, despite federal laws prohibiting them. Members of minority faiths who challenge these practices are vilified, harassed and even threatened with physical injury by their "godly" neighbors.

Considering the persistence of religious bigotry, not to mention the history of religious warfare, it is a bit perverse to promote religion as an antidote for social disorder. Of course religious beliefs must be respected and accommodated—all religious beliefs and the lack of them. Alliances between church and state inevitably lead to the elevation of some beliefs over others, and in public life, religion generates a particularly vicious form of identity politics.

If you imbue religion with any functions and power of the state, you had better pray that the gods will save you from their followers.

> "Faith-based groups nationwide are teaming up with government to confront social ills ranging from welfare dependence to failing schools."

Religious Organizations Can Help Solve Social Problems

Joe Loconte

In the following viewpoint, Joe Loconte describes how religious groups and organizations are making significant progress in many communities in alleviating or preventing social problems such as crime and welfare dependency. Loconte contends that the religious messages imparted by faith-based organizations are integral to their success. Many state and local governments are growing to appreciate the positive contributions religious groups can make, and are enlisting their help in dealing with social welfare concerns. Loconte is a research fellow at the Heritage Foundation, a conservative think tank, and author of *Seducing the Samaritan: How Government Contracts Are Reshaping Social Services*.

As you read, consider the following questions:

1. What examples of work by faith-based organizations does Loconte describe?
2. What compromises have church groups and governments reached on preserving church-state separation while involving religious organizations in public problems, according to the author?
3. How is religion incorporated in Prison Fellowship programs in Texas and other states, according to Loconte?

Excerpted from "The Bully and the Pulpit: A New Model for Church-State Partnerships," by Joe Loconte, *Policy Review*, no. 92, November/December 1998. Reprinted with permission.

Every day by 5 A.M., 90 of the 380 inmates at the Jester II prison outside Houston are awake and primed—not for pumping iron, but for praying. The men, some of whom are violent felons, are enrolled in an intensive Christian rehabilitation program hosted by prison officials. "We talk Jesus every day, every minute," says program director Jack Cowley, "and we don't hide that fact at all." State guards provide security, but volunteers from Prison Fellowship otherwise run this wing of the facility, better known as the God Pod.

In South Carolina, Governor David Beasley used his leftover campaign funds to set up a religious nonprofit group with a singular mission: recruit churches and synagogues to "adopt" welfare families and lift them toward independence. The effort is vigorously backed by the state's Department of Social Services (DSS). "We've done focus groups with clients who've been successful in getting off welfare and we asked them the most important aspect of their success," says Leon Love, a DSS official. "They say it's attitude—and faith is the most important builder of attitude."

At Parkview Elementary School in Washington, D.C., the Reverend Jim Till heads a privately run, faith-based tutoring program. Thursday nights in the cafeteria, volunteers from local churches help about 60 at-risk kids improve their math and reading skills, concluding each session with a story drawn from the Bible. "We're part of the Parkview family," says Till, who calls to mind an affable uncle. "They know exactly what it is we're doing."

What these religious organizations are doing, in fact, is demolishing mistaken assumptions about the separation of church and state—while respecting their constitutional limits. After decades of isolation and suspicion, faith-based groups nationwide are teaming up with government to confront social ills ranging from welfare dependence to failing schools. Agreements are being struck that enlist the active support of government, yet zealously guard the independence of the faithful. "Some officials still look askance at anyone who quotes the Bible," says Marvin Olasky, a University of Texas professor whose books helped propel federal welfare reform. "But many are desperate enough to approve anything that works." Although operating below the radar of the social-service establishment, these partnerships could help redefine the nation's culture of caregiving.

A New Road

Until recently, there appeared to be only two roads for people of faith eager to help the needy: scorn government as a useless annoyance or become paid agents of the secular, administrative state. To be sure, anti-religious legal dogma has scared countless charitable groups away. Yet many cannot resist government largesse, and quickly join those social-service providers already awash in public funding. In Boston, Catholic Charities gets about 65 percent of its budget from state and federal sources. For Lutheran Social Services in New York, the figure is about 80 percent.

Government funding, however, invites government regulation. The U.S. Supreme Court has ruled that the state can subsidize religious charities so long as they are not, in the words of the Court, "pervasively sectarian." This means groups must excise expressions of faith, such as prayer and proselytizing, from their taxpayer-funded programs. Many of them barely retain any distinctive religious identity.

Hence a new *via media* [middle way] in church-state relations: charitable groups that shun Caesar's coin but not Caesar's cooperation. A growing company of religious providers are willing to accept the state's administrative and moral support but forgo its money and oversight. That allows them to tread on secular turf with a message that is, at its heart, religious.

At the same time, deals are being hammered out that satisfy secularists as well as sectarians. Programs contain blunt appeals to moral and spiritual renewal, yet participants are free to opt out. State officials can steer people toward church-based assistance, so long as they offer secular alternatives. Ministers may proselytize clients of government agencies, but not with public money and usually not on public property.

Remarkably, government officials are among those most determined to involve faith communities. Mississippi governor Kirk Fordice was one of the first to challenge churches to help welfare families, and his efforts are being duplicated in at least half a dozen other states. Texas governor George Bush is cutting state regulations that hinder religious groups involved in social services. Indianapolis mayor Stephen Goldsmith has created a "Front Porch Alliance" in which government agencies brainstorm ways to engage congregations in community renewal.

"There are far greater threats to our inner-city children than religion," Goldsmith says. "In many of our most troubled neighborhoods, clearly the most important asset is the church.". . .

Defusing the Crime Bomb

Princeton University criminologist John DiIulio proposes a thought experiment when he lectures on inner-city crime. Imagine, he says, you're driving alone at night through a blighted urban neighborhood. Your car is about to break down, but your guardian angel will allow you to choose one of three places for your car to die. Choice number one: in front of a movie theater where a teen slasher film is about to let out. Choice number two: outside a go-go bar serving malt liquor to underage drinkers. Choice number three: in front of a church resounding with the voices of the youth choir. "Naturally, you're praying for number three," he says. "You simply suppose that people involved with religious institutions are less likely to do you harm."

According to DiIulio, the best social-science research confirms what common sense suggests: Active religious congregations are a critical factor in reducing violence and stabilizing inner-city neighborhoods. A 1991 study published by the National Bureau of Economic Research, for example, found that urban youth whose neighbors attend church are more likely to have a job and less likely to use drugs or commit crime.

This fact is slowly insinuating itself into local crime-fighting strategies. Police are turning to clergy as the eyes and ears of their neighborhoods. Judges and prosecutors are diverting criminals from jail into church-based programs. Ministers and volunteers are invading prisons and bringing a tough-love gospel with them. In all this activity, church and state share at least one goal: lower crime rates through moral rehabilitation. Their challenge is to balance the coercive power of government with respect for offenders' religious beliefs—or lack of them. . . .

Targeting Juvenile Offenders

In Indiana, the Marion County juvenile court sends troubled kids to the Indianapolis Training Center (ITC), a Christian-based alternative to state detention centers. The one-year residential program matches 12- to 18-year-olds with a mentor family and volunteers from local high schools. Although not a lock-down facility, the ITC leaves little time for mischief. Residents are up at 5:30 A.M., usually reading from Proverbs, the Old Testament book stuffed with sound-bite advice on honesty, hard work, and holiness. Mornings are spent doing chores, afternoons studying, and evenings playing sports.

County officials overcame early objections by making sure parents and children understand the regimen. "We will not order anybody into it, but once they choose it, they are ordered to follow through," says Brian Toepp, the county's assistant chief of probation. Moreover, by accepting only private money, ITC is free to immerse its residents in Christian teaching. "We're trying to teach them character," says director Benny McWha, "and we believe character is based on biblical principles.". . .

There are many reasons for the state's willingness to try religious approaches. In Marion County one of them is sheer numbers: Each year the court system sees 10,000 youths and families, far too many for state-paid counselors or probation officers to track. "We have this untapped resource in almost every corner of every neighborhood," Payne says. "But we have virtually excluded churches from the service-delivery system."

No one in Indianapolis makes that point more convincingly than Mayor Stephen Goldsmith. With a lawyer's steely logic, the former prosecutor explains why secular government cannot afford to ignore, much less harass, religious communities. "Only hardened skeptics have trouble accepting that widespread belief in a Supreme Being improves the strength and health of our communities," he says. "Government can accomplish more by working with faith-based groups than it can ever achieve by circumventing them."

Goldsmith's Front Porch Alliance, what he calls a "civic switchboard," probably reigns as the national leader in this regard. In just a few years, the Alliance has developed nearly 600 partnerships while working with more than 150 churches and other value-shaping groups. It also sets up workshops for civic leaders, giving them technical assistance for navigating local bureaucracies or tapping into community resources. . . .

The God Pod

Prison Fellowship's invasion of a Texas prison surely ranks as one of the nation's most audacious experiments in criminal re-habilitation. The program, called Innerchange, is run inside the belly of a state correctional facility. Program staff have 24-hour access to inmates in one wing of the prison, and oversee virtually all day-to-day activities there. Participants need not claim a Christian faith, but must agree to a "Bible-based, Christ-centered" program. Although inmates are allowed to pursue their own religious beliefs (some attend weekly Islamic services), the explicit goal is Christian conversion.

Chaplains have always worked in prisons, of course, but never as comprehensively as Innerchange staff. Says senior warden Fred Becker, "It's the difference between being in church on Sunday and practically being in seminary."

Prison Fellowship may have designed a lawsuit-proof approach to getting God into the nation's prison system: The program is funded purely from private sources, is completely voluntary, has no effect on participants' length of parole, and does not discriminate on the basis of religion. . . .

A Welfare Revolution

Informal agreements between churches and city hall traditionally characterized efforts to help America's poor, until they were eclipsed by the modern welfare state. "Many lives can be saved if we recapture the vision that changed lives up to a century ago, when our concept of compassion was not so corrupt," writes Olasky in *The Tragedy of American Compassion* (1992). The Welfare Reform Act of 1996, which ended the guarantee of federal aid to the poor, may be a step back to the future.

Leon Love, the deputy director of South Carolina's DSS, is unusually frank about his agency's failed welfare policies. "We used to build barriers to prevent churches from participating. We hid behind confidentiality," he says. "But people on the road to self-sufficiency must believe they can get there, and to put a person in the company of believers is powerful."

Views of George W. Bush

Why do some faith-based organizations succeed where secular or government programs fail?

It's because they change hearts. There are faith-based organizations in drug treatment that work so well because they convince a person to turn their life over to Christ. And by doing so, they change the person's heart. A person with a changed heart is less likely to be addicted to drugs and alcohol.

I've had some personal experience with this. As has been reported, I quit drinking. The main reason I quit was because I accepted Jesus Christ into my life in 1986. Billy Graham planted a seed in my heart, and it grew. I believe in the power of faith.

What does society lose if faith-based organizations are marginalized and excluded from partnership with government?

We lose the capacity to have a nation where the American dream touches every willing heart. We lose the capacity of a nation under God.

We have children locked into failing schools. We've got babies being born out of wedlock. We've got drug addiction. We've got 1.2 million children whose parents are in prison. They're six times more likely to commit a crime themselves. By excluding faith-based institutions from addressing these problems, we miss an opportunity to change people's lives for the better.

George W. Bush, interviewed by Deann Alford, *Christianity Today*, October 25, 1999.

In no other area of social policy has the shift in conventional wisdom been more dramatic. Welfare offices are being renamed "family independence agencies." Eligibility experts are scrambling to help recipients find jobs. And congregations are being invited—sometimes begged—to lend a hand.

Governments are turning to religious groups for help in part because they must meet state-imposed deadlines for terminating assistance. But surely the deeper reason is the disastrous failure of welfare to lead families out of poverty. This is especially true for the "hard cases": young mothers with no self-respect, no high-school diploma, and no work history. These are the families whose problems cannot be solved by a booming economy.

Nor, it should be added, by government caseworkers, who spend perhaps an hour a month with welfare recipients. Unraveling the practical and moral problems of these families simply cannot be done on the cheap. "We can do some of that, but we're limited, because we're primarily eligibility specialists," says Elizabeth Seale of the Texas Department of Human Services.

Enter the faith community. "It appears that only churches are willing to make the long-term volunteer investment required," writes Amy Sherman, author of *Restorers of Hope: Reaching the Poor in Your Community with Church-Based Ministries That Work* (1997) and a leading welfare-reform specialist. Thousands of congregations around the country are working closely with welfare families, helping them find jobs, lending emotional support, assisting with child care, and helping with budgeting and even grocery shopping.

It can be labor-intensive work: Churches in Anne Arundel County, Maryland, for example, report that over a six-month period they log an average of 400 hours per family. And not all of that time is spent holding hands: Career counseling usually comes with biblical teachings about work and family responsibilities, placing new moral demands on the poor. . . .

Building Safeguards

States are designing partnerships with congregations that are keeping litigators at bay. For example, no information on welfare recipients is released to churches without their consent. Families must agree to any relationship with a congregation and are never obligated to attend services or church events. State money almost never flows directly to churches, and public assistance usually continues until recipients are independent. "So long as individuals may freely choose religion, merely enabling private decisions logically cannot be a government establishment of religion," writes Carl Esbeck, a law professor at the University of Missouri and a leading authority on the legality of government collaboration with religious groups. . . .

In Michigan, where Governor John Engler's welfare reforms have slashed caseloads, Ottawa County became the first locality in the nation to move every able-bodied welfare recipient into a job. It was one of six sites in the governor's Project Zero, chosen specifically because of its extensive church network.

State officials give much of the credit to the Good Samaritan Center, a church-based nonprofit that recruits and trains church volunteers to support families moving from welfare to work. Within six months of being approached by Engler, Good Samaritan had enlisted nearly 60 churches, or about 25 percent of the county's total. "Determining eligibility—that we do well. We're not very good at wrapping our arms around a family," says Loren Snippe, who oversaw the Ottawa effort. "Church volunteers bring the ability to have a long-term relationship. You can't pay people to do this."

By serving as honest brokers between church and state, . . . nonprofits . . . can help maintain a stable partnership even as state and local governments change hands. "The churches need someone they can trust, who knows their internal culture," says Bill Raymond, a former director of Good Samaritan. "But you also need an independent actor who knows how to engage the powers that be."

Another advantage of the nonprofit model is that it guards the independence of churches as they reach out to the welfare families. The nonprofit's job is to ensure a good match between welfare recipients and congregations; government's role is confined mostly to writing checks and sharing client information. . . .

Reclaiming Compassion

All of this activity, though significant, is occurring in a legal and political culture that, in the words of Yale law professor Stephen Carter, "trivializes religious devotion." Many liberals still treat serious religious belief more as a threat than a cure to the nation's social ills. Writing in the *American Prospect*, Wendy Kaminer called these partnerships an "unholy alliance," suggesting they are part of a larger campaign "to align public policies with majoritarian religious practices and ideals."

Too many government officials see the same dark conspiracies. A few years ago, Indianapolis mayor Goldsmith asked churches to participate in a summer job-training program. At the end of the summer, the state of Indiana cited the city as "out of compliance" with a state law barring the use of funds for religious purposes. The reason: Participants voluntarily prayed before meals and field trips.

Many in government, however, are unpersuaded by the yowling of liberal legalists. "We have a common goal," says Milton Britton, the chief probation officer of Massachusetts. "We're trying to improve the quality of life for our communities. When you bring the moral perspective, the anchor that prevents you from falling off the edge, it makes a difference."

Until the onset of the modern welfare state, the decisive power of faith to curb evil and inspire charity was taken for granted. Even French philosopher Voltaire, a relentless critic of Christianity, argued that societies would collapse into disorder without some type of rational religion. "I want my attorney, my tailor, my servants, even my wife to believe in God," he said, "and I think that then I shall be robbed and cuckolded less often."

Ironically, it is the welfare bureaucracy's moral collapse that has lawmakers and others taking another look at the faith community. . . .

Religious believers and broad-minded lawmakers are ratifying an old precept of American civic life: that collaboration between church and state need not lead to corruption. They are steering their way around those who fret over a lunchtime prayer, as well as those who would trade their souls for a government contract. And they follow Goldsmith's golden rule of government: "We will never ask an organization to change any of its core values in order to participate in a relationship with us."

With that rule to guide them—and with a little faith, hope, and charity—they might just reclaim and sanctify the compassionate impulses of a new generation of caregivers.

"To ascribe to faith-based organizations a magical power to heal all social ills is to forget how limited their resources are and always will be."

Religious Organizations Cannot Solve Social Problems

Jacob S. Hacker

A growing number of politicians advocate the involvement of religious or "faith-based" organizations in helping juvenile delinquents, prisoners, and families attempting to get off welfare, notes Jacob S. Hacker in the following viewpoint. However, Hacker questions the efficacy of such groups and whether private religious groups can truly replace the government in providing for the social welfare of people in need. Hacker researches and writes about social welfare policy for the New America Foundation, a public policy institute.

As you read, consider the following questions:
1. Why are so many politicians calling for increased government reliance on religious organizations, according to Hacker?
2. What differences does the author describe between conservative and liberal advocates of faith-based organizations?
3. How much money is spent on government social programs compared with that spent by religious institutions, according to Hacker?

Reprinted, with permission, from "Faith Healers," by Jacob S. Hacker, *The New Republic*, June 28, 1999. Reprinted by permission of *The New Republic*; © 1999, The New Republic, Inc.

S peaking at a Salvation Army center in Atlanta in May 1999, Al Gore announced his support of expanded government subsidies for religious groups that were using the "unique power of faith" to fight America's social ills. With his heavily promoted speech, Gore prominently allied himself with an idea that has, until recently, been associated with the "compassionate conservatism" his leading Republican rival [in the 2000 presidential election], Texas Governor George W. Bush, champions.

Of course, Gore and Bush are only two of the growing number of politicians from both parties who have called for increased government reliance on the social welfare activities of churches and religious charities—or what supporters like to call "faith-based organizations." The list includes . . . countless governors, mayors, and state legislators. In Congress, the movement even has its own advocacy coalition: the Renewal Alliance, a bicameral collection of roughly 30 Republicans organized by former Indiana Senator Dan Coats. Beyond Capitol Hill, it has supporters everywhere from the Heritage Foundation to the Brookings Institution.

That the faith-based agenda is so wildly popular is not altogether surprising. It promises to attack poverty and other social problems not by spending more but by freeing public dollars from the clutches of government bureaucrats and shifting them into the hands of religious institutions. As such, it appeals both to conservatives who wish to downsize the welfare state and to liberals who want to foster grassroots solutions to lingering social problems. But it would be a mistake to read too much into this consensus, for behind it remain two very different visions for the future of the welfare state—one of which, at least, is not as appealing as it might sound at first blush.

Liberal and Conservative Visions

Left and right have arrived at this apparent meeting of the minds by strikingly different paths. Recent liberal support for faith-based programs grew out of the Bill Clinton [presidential] administration's effort to stake out a "Third Way" that combines traditional Democratic goals with greater emphasis on personal responsibility and community values.

Since his 1996 declaration that "the era of big government is over," Clinton has been at the forefront of the push for small-scale government interventions designed to enforce widely shared values. Clinton has also been a leading booster of voluntarism and community service, and he has supported efforts to promote cooperation between federal agencies and grassroots organizations. Symbolically appealing yet relatively inexpensive initiatives such as this have been central to Clinton's strategy for rebuilding public faith in government and the Democratic Party, and they would likely play the same role in a Gore administration.

But, even today, for all the talk about downsizing the public sector, liberals do not see faith-based organizations as a substitute for government. Quite the contrary, they believe that government and religious charities should coexist and nurture one another—that they are necessary partners in the strengthening of civil society. (Harvard political scientist Robert Putnam, for example, has argued that carefully tailored public policy can invigorate associations and civic networks.) Not coincidentally, their calls for expanding the role of religious institutions comes in the context of calls for more, not less, spending on social welfare.

Conservatives, by contrast, embrace faith-based organizations as an outright alternative to what they ridicule as the clumsy and permissive top-down welfare policies of the past. Echoing moralists such as Marvin Olasky and Gertrude Himmelfarb, they argue that the welfare state has crippled private charity and compassion, which remain the only effective ways to deal with the nation's social problems. Not only should government do less, but social policy must also be, in Himmelfarb's memorable phrase, "remoralized." It's not enough for government to encourage better values; those in need should be forced to conform with community norms, to take responsibility for their failures, to change inside before expecting outside help. Olasky's 1992 book, *The Tragedy of American Compassion*, extols the private relief efforts of the nineteenth century for demanding personal transformation as a condition of aid. "There was a hardness in those days," Olasky writes approvingly, "based on the belief that some individuals needed to suffer in order to be willing to change."

While this strand of conservative thought seems at odds with the familiar libertarian strand in conservative philosophy, it still comes down in favor of reducing the size of government. Indeed, compassionate conservatives frequently seek to cut back public spending and revenues. For example, former Senator Coats's much-heralded 1996 plan for an expanded charitable tax deduction—one prototype for faith-based-services legislation—would have cost tens of billions of dollars, paid for by cuts in existing social programs. The Renewal Alliance in Congress supports a similar initiative that would allow states to pay for expanded tax breaks for charity by siphoning off up to half of their welfare block grants. These proposals do not represent a new antipoverty crusade so much as they do a renewed push to privatize public responsibilities—or to abdicate them altogether.

As long as the issue at hand involves shifting relatively modest amounts of money, these different agendas don't really matter. Giving a slightly greater role to religious institutions is harmless, maybe even beneficial, and something on which both sides can agree. But liberals will naturally grow suspicious as conservatives push to off-load ever-greater portions of the welfare burden onto faith-based groups. They will argue that this represents a wholesale change in the philosophy of the welfare state, one that would jeopardize the well-being of the people who rely on it. And, based on the available evidence, they will be right to do so.

How Effective Are Faith-Based Programs?

To begin with, it remains an open question just how effective faith-based organizations really would be in a greatly expanded role. Those who champion faith-based programs tend to cite the same familiar examples—Eugene Rivers's Azusa Christian Community in Boston, which has spearheaded community efforts to revitalize inner-city Boston; or Charles Colson's Prison Fellowship ministry, which provides faith-based counseling in prisons across the nation. But systematic research on these and similar programs is meager. And, although some evidence suggests the power of the "faith factor," studies of faith-based programs suffer from the methodological difficulty that many of the programs deemed most successful are small and idiosyncratic, hindering comparison or generalization. Worse, evaluations of faith-based programs inevitably confront the problem of self-selection: people who turn to faith-based charities are likely to be particularly receptive to the message they deliver. The failure of most studies to control adequately for personal and social characteristics that might be associated with participation in faith-based programs makes it hard to know if faith is the key ingredient of these programs' successes, or if faith-based interventions could be replicated on a broader scale.

Reprinted by permission of Joel Kauffmann.

Even if faith-based programs do prove broadly effective, the current scale and scope of these programs means they are, in all likelihood, incapable of bearing too ambitious a burden. State, local, and federal spending on social programs was more than $1.4 trillion in 1994. And this figure does not even include the scores of tax breaks and credit subsidies that have social welfare aims or the extensive spending channeled through private health insurance and other employer-provided benefits—which, all told, would perhaps double the official figure. In contrast, the annual private social spending by congregations, national faith-based charities like the Salvation Army, and other religious organizations is probably not more than $15 billion to $20 billion per year, according to research supported by the nonpartisan Aspen Institute. This is by no means a trivial amount, and it does not account for unpaid volunteer work. But, even if the total contribution of religious organizations was several times larger than the best current estimates, it would still be tiny compared with government spending. To expect institutions of this scope to dramatically expand their infrastructure and expertise in response to new government grants—much less to become the nation's core providers of social assistance—is unrealistic.

The Needs of Poor Communities

Nor are the limited resources controlled by faith-based organizations distributed evenly across American communities. A common theme of recent encomiums to faith-based charities is that their activities are most valuable and vibrant in the poorest inner-city communities. They may well be, but, perversely, the resources available to religious organizations are most limited precisely where the need is greatest. Although the pattern of giving to religious charities is complex, the rate of private donation is generally higher in wealthier communities and lower where social conditions are worse. Larger and wealthier congregations provide services more often, and the congregations most likely to be involved in service provision are in the suburbs, not the inner cities. Even accounting for the long tradition of community outreach in urban African American churches, faith-based organizations in poorer communities still have great trouble raising the private funds necessary to support their programs, particularly as they face far more pervasive and immediate needs. For more than a decade, moreover, the share of private religious giving that is slated for activities not directly tied to a local church has fallen, making the problem of community resource disparities all the more pressing.

Indeed, many faith-based programs active in low-income neighborhoods must already rely on another source for help, and it's the very source many conservatives want to downsize: the government. As Johns Hopkins University political scientist Lester Salamon has argued in a series of influential studies, cooperation between government and nonprofit service providers—including religiously affiliated nonprofits—is a longstanding and pervasive feature of U.S. social policy. Although churches themselves have not been prominent recipients of government funds, many collaborate with local agencies in other ways, sharing information and even providing volunteers for public programs. More important, many religiously affiliated organizations—from national religious networks such as Catholic Charities USA to local faith-based initiatives—do receive government funds, either directly or through separate nonprofit organizations specifically chartered to deliver social services. Catholic Charities USA, for example, receives more than 60 percent of its funding from federal, state, and local governments. Among nonprofit human service providers as a whole, the government now supplies a greater share of operating funds than does private giving. And these funds come on top of the significant tax advantage enjoyed by nonprofit organizations and Americans who donate to them.

The Limits of Religious Organizations

None of this is to deny the immense value of faith-based organizations or to say that they cannot play a somewhat larger role in our social welfare strategy. But to ascribe to faith-based organizations a magical power to heal all social ills is to forget how limited their resources are and always will be, how insufficient their activities were before the arrival of the welfare state and still are today, and how extensively their success depends on a steady supply of public funds and interaction with government agencies. It is also to forget that the strength of many of these institutions rests precisely on their voluntary character—and on their ability to advance beliefs that are sectarian, exclusionary, and even offensive to some. It's not surprising that many conservatives who have long wanted to scale back government believe that faith-based programs can do nearly everything the state now does, only better. What's surprising is that so many people are taking the idea seriously.

"America's faith-based charities . . . have moved people successfully from dependency and despair to the dignity of self-reliance."

The Government Should Fund Faith-Based Social Services

John Ashcroft

John Ashcroft was elected by Missouri voters to the U.S. Senate in 1994. He authored the "charitable choice" provision of the 1996 Welfare Reform Act that allowed state governments to utilize private religious organizations to administer and deliver public welfare services. In 1998 and again in 1999 Ashcroft introduced legislation that would apply a similar rule encouraging religious group participation in all government programs in which nongovernmental bodies are contracted to deliver federally-funded services, including drug abuse treatment, juvenile services, and public housing. The following viewpoint is taken from his May 7, 1998 speech in the Senate. Ashcroft praises the work of religious groups working with welfare recipients, and argues that cooperation between government and religious bodies is necessary to help solve America's social ills. Ashcroft was appointed attorney general by President George W. Bush in 2001.

As you read, consider the following questions:
1. What protections exist for religious organizations that seek public funding for welfare services and for welfare service recipients, according to Ashcroft?
2. What examples of successful work by faith-based organizations does the author describe?

Reprinted from John Ashcroft's speech before the U.S. Senate, *Congressional Record*, May 7, 1998.

For years, America's charities and churches have been transforming shattered lives by addressing the deeper needs of people—by instilling hope and values which help change behavior and attitudes. By contrast, government social programs have failed miserably in moving recipients from dependency and despair to responsibility and independence.

Charitable Choice

Successful faith-based organizations now have a new opportunity to transform the character of our welfare system under the 'Charitable Choice' provision contained in the 1996 welfare reform law. Charitable Choice allows—but does not require—states to contract with charitable, religious or private organizations, or to create voucher systems, to deliver welfare services within the states. The provision requires states to consider these organizations on an equal basis with other private groups once a state decides to use nongovernmental organizations.

The Charitable Choice legislation provides specific protections for religious organizations when they provide services. For example, the government cannot discriminate against an organization on the basis of its religious character. A participating faith-based organization retains its independence from government, including control over the definition, development, practice, and expression of its religious beliefs.

Additionally, the government cannot require a religious organization to alter its form of internal governance or remove religious art, icons, or symbols to be eligible to participate. Finally, religious organizations may consider religious beliefs and practices in their employment decisions.

The Charitable Choice legislation also provides specific protections to beneficiaries of assistance. A religious organization can't discriminate against a beneficiary on account of religion. And if a beneficiary objects to receiving services from a religious organization, he or she has a right to an alternate provider.

Finally, there is a limitation on use of government funds. Federal contract dollars cannot be used for sectarian worship, instruction, or proselytization.

Inspiring Examples

I would like to give a couple of examples of how the Charitable Choice provision of the welfare law is currently working.

Last fall [1997], Payne Memorial Outreach Center, the non-profit community development arm of the 100-year-old Payne Memorial African Methodist Episcopal Church, in Baltimore, received a $1.5 million state contract to launch an innovative job training and placement program. In a matter of only five months, over 100 welfare recipients successfully obtained employment through their participation in Payne's program. A brochure from this dynamic faith-based institution describes why Payne is successful: 'The Intensive Job Service Program reaches out in love to Baltimore's most disenfranchised, helping them to identify and strengthen their God-given talents—releasing and developing their human possibilities.'

Another example of Charitable Choice at work is in Shreveport, Louisiana, where the 'Faith and Families' program, under a contract with the state, is running a successful job placement program. Faith and Families offers job-readiness classes in northwestern Louisiana, helps set up job interviews, and opens doors into the workplace.

The program also links welfare families with faith communities. Churches are asked to adopt a family and provide assistance—possibly child care, transportation, work experience, tutoring, and encouragement—that will help them make the transition from welfare to work.

I spoke with the director of Faith and Families in Shreveport just last week [in May 1998], and he told me that his organization has helped 400 people get off welfare and find jobs.

These examples demonstrate that under the Charitable Choice provision of the welfare law, caring, faith-based organizations are providing effective services that help individuals move from dependency to independence, from despair to dignity.

Expanding Charitable Choice

With this in mind, I am introducing 'The Charitable Choice Expansion Act of 1998,' which expands the Charitable Choice concept to all federal laws which authorize the government to use non-governmental entities to provide services to beneficiaries with federal dollars.

The substance of the Charitable Choice Expansion Act is virtually identical to that of the original Charitable Choice provision of the welfare reform law. The only real difference between the two provisions is that the new bill covers many more federal programs than the original provision.

Why Religious Organizations Succeed

We have Catholic schools that are educating youngsters in inner cities where the public schools are failing. We have churches that are rescuing people from drug abuse and homelessness in places where public social services are failing. Religion-based organizations (some, at least) are succeeding because they are able to reach that inner part of their clients that is off-limits to the government.

As things now stand, the government can neither do what these faith-based organizations demonstrably can do nor fund their doing it. Some efforts to split the difference come off as ludicrous—as when Michigan contracted with the Salvation Army to provide services for the homeless but required it to forgo its spiritual ministry. The result was to render the Salvation Army effort no more successful than the government effort it replaced.

Is there no way out? Kevin J. Hasson believes there is: Let the government provide resources for individuals, and let those individuals use the resources where they will. Surely the Constitution doesn't forbid the government to help people.

William Raspberry, *Washington Post*, July 10, 2000.

While the original Charitable Choice provision applies mainly to the new welfare reform block grant program, the Charitable Choice Expansion Act applies to all federal government programs in which the government is authorized to use nongovernmental organizations to provide federally funded services to beneficiaries. Some of the programs that will be covered include: housing, substance abuse prevention and treatment, juvenile services, seniors services, the Community Development Block Grant, the Community Services Block Grant, the Social Services Block Grant, abstinence education, and child welfare services.

The legislation does not cover elementary and secondary education programs . . . or higher education programs. Further, the bill does not affect the Head Start program or the Child Care Development Block Grant program, both of which already contain certain provisions regarding the use of religious organizations in delivering services under those programs.

More Protections

We have taken measures to strengthen the bill by providing more protections to both beneficiaries and religious organizations. For example, the government must ensure that beneficiaries receive notice of their right under the bill to object to receiving services from a religious organization. Additionally, religious organizations must segregate their own private funds from government funding.

This proposal is necessary because while some areas of the law may not contain discriminatory language towards religious organizations, many government officials may assume wrongly that the Establishment Clause [of the First Amendment] bars religious organizations from participating as private providers.

The Charitable Choice Expansion Act embodies existing case precedents to clarify to government officials and religious organizations alike that it is constitutionally allowable, and even constitutionally required, to consider religious organizations on an equal basis with other private providers. It is my hope that these protections in the law will encourage successful charitable and faith-based organizations to expand their services while assuring them that they will not have to extinguish their religious character when receiving government funds.

I am pleased to say that there is broad-based support for the Charitable Choice Expansion Act. Some of the organizations supporting the concept of this legislation include Agudath Israel, American Center for Law and Justice, Call to Renewal, Center for Public Justice, Christian Coalition, Christian Legal Society, the Coalition on Urban Renewal and Education, National Association of Evangelicals, the National Center for Neighborhood Enterprise, the Salvation

Army, Teen Challenge International USA, and World Vision.

America's faith-based charities and nongovernmental organizations, from the Salvation Army to Catholic Charities, have moved people successfully from dependency and despair to the dignity of self-reliance. Government alone will never cure our societal ills. We need to find ways to help unleash the cultural remedy administered so effectively by charitable and religious organizations. Allowing a 'charitable choice' will help transform the lives of those in need and unleash an effective response to today's challenges in our culture.

"Charitable choice' initiatives . . . are unconstitutional, bad public policy and fundamentally bad for religion."

The Government Should Not Fund Faith-Based Social Services

Anti-Defamation League

In 1996, Congress passed welfare reform legislation that included a "charitable choice" provision authorizing taxpayer funding for religious organizations to deliver certain welfare services such as job training. Religious groups no longer had to establish separate secularized agencies to qualify for government funding. Some politicians have proposed that religious groups should be allowed to receive public money to deliver services in other federal government programs. In the following viewpoint, the Anti-Defamation League (ADL) argues that although many religious organizations are helping people in need, giving government money to religious groups for social services jeopardizes the integrity of recipient religious institutions and subjects people to religious coercion. The ADL is an international organization that works to combat anti-Semitism and other forms of bigotry and discrimination.

As you read, consider the following questions:
1. How does government funding of religious groups create religious coercion, according to the authors?
2. What alternative to "charitable choice" provisions does ADL support?

Proponents of religious freedom in America have long recognized that government and religion make poor bedfellows. As [former Supreme Court] Justice Hugo Black observed, "a union of government and religion tends to destroy government and degrade religion." In recent years, however, legislators at both the Federal and state levels have been proposing initiatives that fly in the face of this hard-earned lesson. Like many bad ideas, these initiatives often have names that offer no hint of their real impact. One such bad idea has been dubbed "charitable choice" by its supporters.

The Federal "charitable choice" measure, which was first adopted in 1996 as part of the welfare reform bill, mandates that whenever the Federal Government allows private organizations to assist in the distribution of welfare benefits, the Government must also allow religious organizations and sectarian institutions, which integrate religious practices into their programs, to have an equal opportunity to participate. If the Federal Government decides to let a private organization provide counseling services, for example, then the Government must also consider the bids of religious institutions when deciding with whom to contract.

A growing number of politicians currently favor an expanded church-state partnership in a wide range of social welfare activities. Some who support "charitable choice" do so in an effort to downsize the Government's commitment to anti-poverty programs or as part of an effort to shift the cost of providing such services to faith-based organizations. Legislation has been introduced in Congress to extend the "charitable choice" concept beyond welfare programs to such areas as job training, juvenile delinquency prevention initiatives, and drug rehabilitation programs. Further, numerous similar programs, also calling themselves "charitable choice," have been introduced in state legislatures across the country.

Even in these days of unprecedented prosperity, millions of Americans live in poverty and must meet the challenge of getting by—not to mention moving up in the world—with little assistance from the Government. ADL recognizes that, while state and Federally funded programs like food stamps and welfare provide much needed assistance to the nation's poor, many families rely on charities—including those affiliated with religious organizations. In many inner cities, some of the most effective groups making a real difference in the lives of the community are religious institutions, whose outreach programs provide food, shelter and counseling to even the most destitute.

Nonetheless, ADL opposes "charitable choice" initiatives because we believe that they are unconstitutional, bad public policy and fundamentally bad for religion.

Government Funding for Religious-Affiliated Organizations

Government funding for religious organizations providing social services is not new. Under current law, government support for religiously affiliated soup kitchens, homeless shelters, counseling and job-training programs is reflected in the provision of tax benefits for certain individual and corporate charitable contributions. In addition, religiously affiliated social service agencies, such as Lutheran Social Services, Catholic Charities and Jewish Federations, receive very substantial direct government subsidies for providing a variety of quasi-governmental services if they operate under certain structural restrictions which guard against the possibility of any religious coercion. These separately incorporated, religious-affiliated organizations have played an essential role in combating poverty and providing housing, education and health care services to the poor, elderly, homeless and other people in need.

"Charitable Choice" Is Unconstitutional

Before the passage of "charitable choice," in order to receive government funding, religious organizations were required to establish firewalls between their social service initiatives and their sectarian mission programs to ensure that these services were provided without a specific religious message and with appropriate constitutional safeguards. Previously, religious organizations had to establish a separately incorporated agency and offer services to all without regard to religious belief, and were not permitted to discriminate in the hiring of staff.

"Charitable choice" programs plainly violate the First

Amendment's prohibition against funding that promotes religious beliefs. Allowing sectarian institutions to take the place of government as the provider of essential services in a community will likely result in the kind of coercion that the [First Amendment's] Establishment Clause was designed to prevent.

Questioning Assumptions About Faith-Based Services

As the situation unfolds, certain assumptions have been made that may not be entirely accurate. For example, proponents of government funding for faith-based social services claim that religious groups do a better job of providing this assistance than government agencies. However, there is little, if any, objective research that supports this claim.

Substance abuse treatment programs are an oft-cited example. People who run faith-based alcohol and drug addiction recovery programs claim high rates of success and assert that only religion can motivate addicts to change their behavior.

But critics are skeptical. "To my knowledge there is no empirical research that supports those claims," says William McColl, director of government relations for the National Association of Alcoholism and Drug Abuse Counselors, based in Arlington, Va. "There are incredible claims of 80 percent recovery rates [by religious providers], but they are not empirical studies, and they have not been done by objective researchers. We can go tit for tat with the anecdotal evidence; everyone has anecdotal evidence."

McColl does not doubt that religion can play an important role in substance abuse recovery, but he is wary of "charitable choice" schemes because they might encourage religious organizations to set up addiction programs staffed by people who do not have the proper training in the field.

Says McColl, "It's a question of providing safe, professional care to the client so they know their health care is in good hands."

Rob Boston, *Church and State*, February 1998.

"Charitable choice" threatens to subject a large segment of American society to religious coercion—at taxpayers' expense. Needy citizens may be directed to religious institutions where they may feel pressured to participate in religious practice or proselytization in order to receive their benefits. "Charitable choice" could result, for example, in Jewish families being encouraged to listen to Christian evangelists in order to receive government assistance.

Although many of society's most needy are likely to be the least informed about their rights—including their right under "charitable choice" to request another benefit site—the law does not require that service providers inform beneficiaries of their right to attend non-religious programs. A drug addict seeking court-ordered rehabilitation counseling may be directed toward a faith-based program without understanding that he has the option of attending a secular alternative instead. Once in the program, he may keep quiet about his own beliefs rather than risk being sent back to jail.

"Charitable Choice" Is Bad Public Policy

"Charitable choice" explicitly creates, for the first time, the possibility of Federally-funded employment discrimination on the basis of religion. Since religious institutions are exempt from the nondiscrimination requirements of Title VII and other anti-discrimination laws, "charitable choice" essentially amounts to a form of government-subsidized religious discrimination. For example, a Presbyterian Church receiving funds for a welfare program could refuse to hire non-Presbyterians to administer the program. Further, even racist or anti-Semitic groups—such as the Nation of Islam or Christian Identity—may be able to receive Federal money to provide benefits and services.

As they do under current law, religious institutions that receive Federal funds under "charitable choice" programs should be required to comply with the same standards and regulations that currently govern existing social service agencies. These necessary quality-control requirements may include professional training standards, disability access requirements, and health, safety, and fire regulations.

"Charitable Choice" Is Bad for Religion

Finally, "charitable choice" threatens the health of American religious institutions themselves. Religion has thrived in America precisely because the government is prohibited from endorsing or burdening religious practice. "Charitable choice" raises serious concerns about the possibility of government entanglement with religious practices and is likely to result in unwelcome, divisive competition among religious groups before elected officials for scarce government funds. Many religious organizations have been rightly wary of "charitable choice," concerned that their religious ministries would be subject to intrusive government regulation, including audits, reporting requirements and compliance reviews.

On one hand, the specter of government inspectors monitoring those funded programs that take place in houses of worship is deeply disturbing. On the other hand, "charitable choice" would also seem to require religious people—many who have devoted their lives to spreading a spiritual message through words and good deeds—to muzzle themselves about their most fundamental beliefs while attempting to fulfill a deeply spiritual mission. Many religions are by their very nature evangelical; to require that their adherents not proselytize in these programs clearly dilutes their spiritual missions—ultimately compromising their intended power to inspire and uplift their beneficiaries.

Moreover, churches and synagogues have traditionally provided a wide array of community health and welfare services as part of their sacred religious missions. They have been supported by the countless hours of volunteer services and social action by members of their congregations and communities. Receipt of government funds may have a negative impact on volunteer contributions and involvement of church members. Receipt of Federal funds and fierce competition for scarce resources may also compromise religion's historic role as an independent social critic.

"Charitable choice" allows for an unprecedented entanglement of government and religion—to the detriment of both. Rather than abandon our nation's great tradition of separation of church and state which has allowed religion to flourish in the United States, the Government should encourage increased private subsidies for religious ministries, including tax incentives for charitable contributions. Every needy American should be able to receive help without being subjected to religious coercion.

Periodical Bibliography

The following articles have been selected to supplement the diverse views presented in this chapter. Addresses are provided for periodicals not indexed in the *Readers' Guide to Periodical Literature*, the *Alternative Press Index*, the *Social Sciences Index*, or the *Index to Legal Periodicals and Books*.

Jodie T. Allen	"Ministers Test the Limits of Faith," *U.S. News & World Report*, January 3–10, 2000.
Cheryl Henderson Blunt	"Networking Against Poverty," *Christianity Today*, April 3, 2000.
Franz Buggle et al.	"Are Atheists More Depressed than Religious People?" *Free Inquiry*, Fall 2000. Available from PO Box 664, Amherst, NY 14226-0664.
Christianity Today	"Bush's Faith-Based Plans," October 25, 1999.
E.J. Dionne	"Religion and the Future of the American Experiment," *American Outlook*, Summer 2000.
Futurist	"Welfare May Spark Church-State Conflict," April 1999.
Dennis R. Hoover	"Yes to Charitable Choice," *Nation*, August 7–14, 2000.
Michael Kazin and John Copeland	"Faith in Labor," *Nation*, October 11, 1999.
Joe Loconte	"Leap of Faith," *National Review*, July 12, 1999.
Richard Parker	"Progressive Politics and, uh, . . . God," *American Prospect*, January 17, 2000.
Amy L. Sherman	"Churches as Government Partners: Navigating 'Charitable Choice,'" *Christian Century*, July 5–12, 2000.
Tim Stafford	"The Criminologist Who Discovered Churches," *Christianity Today*, June 14, 1999.
Andrew Sullivan	"Armies of Confusion," *New Republic*, July 7, 2000.
James Q. Wilson	"Religion and Public Life," *Brookings Review*, Spring 1999.
Frank R. Zindler	"Religion and Violence," *American Atheist*, Summer 1999.

CHAPTER 3

What Should Be Done to Accommodate Religious Freedom in America?

Chapter Preface

Religious freedom has long been an important value in American society. Its significance can be seen in the fact that the First Amendment of the Bill of Rights begins: "Congress shall make no law respecting an establishment of religion, or prohibiting the free exercise thereof." These clauses at first applied only to Congress and federal laws, but in the 1940s the Supreme Court ruled that they also applied to state and local laws.

The practical application of the First Amendment's clauses on religious freedom has been the source of much debate. In recent years, Congress and the Supreme Court have considered whether people should be exempt from laws that are in conflict with their religious beliefs—even if the laws are not specifically directed against religion.

The 1990 case of *Employment Division v. Smith* concerned state employees who had been fired and denied unemployment compensation after breaking drug laws. The employees, who were followers of the Native American Church, argued that they had consumed the hallucinogen peyote as part of their religious observances, and that their freedom of religion was being unconstitutionally infringed. A majority of Supreme Court justices disagreed, ruling that religious claims cannot be used to justify violating laws with a general "rational" application but whose "incidental effect" limited religious freedom. This marked a reversal from prior Supreme Court rulings in which the Court found that only "compelling interests" justified the passing of laws that created burdens on a person's free exercise of religion.

The *Employment Division v. Smith* ruling surprised and angered many supporters of religious freedom. In 1993 Congress passed the Religious Freedom Restoration Act, which was meant to restore the "compelling interest" test to laws affecting religious exercise, but the Supreme Court declared the legislation unconstitutional in 1997. Some states have also created religious exemptions to various laws. The viewpoints in this chapter examine the debate over how far the law, and American society in general, should go to accommodate religious beliefs and practices.

"It is long overdue . . . that we correct the decisions that the U.S. Supreme Court has heaped upon us."

The U.S. Constitution Should Be Amended to Protect Religious Liberty

Ernest Istook

Ernest Istook is a Republican representative of Oklahoma in the U.S. House of Representatives. In 1997 he introduced legislation calling on Congress to enact a "Religious Freedom Amendment" to the U.S. Constitution. In the following viewpoint, taken from remarks on the House floor in 1998, Istook explains what his amendment is meant to accomplish and why he believes it to be necessary. He contends that religious freedom in America as envisioned by the writers of the Constitution has been compromised by Supreme Court decisions that have banned organized prayer in schools, religious displays on public property, and other instances of religious practice. The Constitution must be amended to clearly establish and protect the rights of all people to practice their religion, he asserts. Istook's amendment won a majority in a June 4, 1998, vote, but fell short of the two-thirds necessary to amend the Constitution.

As you read, consider the following questions:
1. What Supreme Court decisions does Istook criticize?
2. What is the proper understanding of the phrase "separation of church and state," according to the author?
3. What precedents exist for placing the word "God" in the U.S. Constitution, according to Istook?

Reprinted from Ernest Istook's remarks before the U.S. House of Representatives, *Congressional Record*, March 10, 1998.

I wanted to take the time this evening to talk about one of the most significant problems that has plagued America because of a multitude of Supreme Court decisions, which the American people have never accepted. You see, there is a problem with lack of respect for our Constitution and for the history and the heritage which brought our Constitution to us.

In fact, what brought so many people to America originally was their desire for religious freedom. We look at the stories of the Pilgrims and Puritans, and we recognize that they were motivated by a desire to be in a land where they could be free to worship as they pleased to worship. And that has been so much of the bedrock of American values, but it has been under attack by the United States Supreme Court.

Unfortunate Supreme Court Decisions

In 1962, the Supreme Court said [that] . . . students could not come together and pray at school the way that they had since the founding of the republic. In 1998, the U.S. Supreme Court said the Ten Commandments could not be on the wall of the public school because, and this is what the U.S. Supreme Court said, the students might read and obey the Ten Commandments. So, thanks to the court, of course, our students do not read the Ten Commandments and certainly there is a problem in getting people to obey them.

In 1985, the U.S. Supreme Court said even a moment of silence was wrong. A law to permit a moment of silence, they declared, was unconstitutional because it . . . [implied that it] was okay for students to use that time to pray silently.

In 1992, the Supreme Court said that a rabbi broke the law by offering prayer at a public school graduation. And in 1995, the same Supreme Court, which has ruled that a Nazi swastika is protected on public policy, ruled that a cross could not be included in a group of symbols on a city seal to show the heritage of that community. . . .

That is the same Supreme Court that had said that you could not have a nativity scene in Pennsylvania in Allegheny County. They said a nativity scene, or for that matter a menorah, were unconstitutional because they were not sufficiently balanced by emblems like Santa Claus and Frosty the Snowman and the reindeer. Because of that, they said it was unconstitutional to have the Christmas displays that so many places have had. . . .

These decisions started in 1962. There is a whole series of them. I have not even mentioned all of them. But . . . the time has come to end the judicial misinterpretations of the U.S. Constitution.

The first amendment says, "Congress shall make no law respecting an establishment of religion or prohibiting the free exercise thereof." But the Supreme Court has misconstrued that to say, "Oh, well, if you have a prayer at public school, that is the same thing as establishing an official church." Of course it is not.

The Religious Freedom Amendment

Common sense tells us it is not, but it is used by people who are intolerant of religion. That is why over 150 members of this body, of the House of Representatives, have so far joined together with me in sponsoring the religious freedom amendment. It is a proposed amendment to the U.S. Constitution to tell the Supreme Court it is time that we straighten out these things. . . .

The text . . . of the religious freedom amendment is pretty straightforward. I would like to share it with members. It reads,

> To secure the people's right to acknowledge God according to the dictates of conscience, neither the United States nor any State shall establish any official religion, but the people's right to pray and to recognize their religious beliefs, heritage or traditions on public property, including schools, shall not be infringed. The government shall not require any person to join in prayer or other religious activity, prescribe school prayers, discriminate against religion or deny equal access to a benefit on account of religion.

It is pretty simple. It is pretty straightforward. It expresses that we have a right to acknowledge God in America according to the dictates of our own conscience, and neither the United States nor any State is to establish any official religion. Government is not going to tell us how to believe or what faith we must profess or indeed if we must profess any faith, but the people have a right to pray, even when they are on public property, and that is an individual right and a collective right. We can do it as individuals. We can do it as a group. Government can accommodate that and make it possible for it to occur. And also if it is a recognition of religious belief, heritage or tradition, that is okay. . . .

Discrimination Against Religion

And we have a protection in the religious freedom amendment. You are not going to discriminate against religion and you are not going to deny equal access to a benefit on account of religion.

I recall in Oklahoma City . . . after the [1995 terrorist] bombing and when there was Federal assistance to rebuild the area of downtown Oklahoma City damaged by the blast of the Murrah Building, there were hundreds of other structures that also suffered damage in that. Several of them within a block or two of the blast were churches. The Department of Housing and Urban Development had to get their arms twisted . . . to accept the idea that a church, just like any other business or enterprise or building nearby, could receive the rebuilding assistance that came from the Federal Government to the properties damaged by the Murrah Building blast. I think that is proper.

We do not say that we are going to help this building over here because it is a copy business or a printing business or a restaurant but, oh, we will help everybody except those that are institutions of faith. We are not going to pay them for their religion or for their religious ceremonies, but we are going to treat them equally if there is some sort of Federal assistance program. Because churches are involved in so many things; they are involved in welfare assistance, they are involved in housing assistance, they are involved in programs against drinking and drugs and rehabilitation. Why should we say that when we have a Federal grant that is available to help somebody get on the right track again, if they have a spiritual component as part of their program, they are going to be disqualified?

The religious freedom amendment is not about supporting churches. . . . But when they have a program that meshes with what we are trying to accomplish to help people get on the right track . . . you do not disqualify someone.

Just like, for example, take Federal education assistance. . . . We do not tell somebody, look, if you go to the University of Oklahoma or the University of Virginia or the University of Michigan, you can have the Federal assistance in education. Oh, but if you are going to go to Notre Dame or some other Catholic institution, or if you go to Baylor, which is where I went to college, since it is a Baptist institution, you cannot do that. Or Brigham Young or Southern Methodist, we do not say that we are going to disqualify you because you are going to a school that has a religious affiliation. No, we understand that the purpose is education.

So the religious freedom amendment also seeks to cut down on the attacks that people are making, trying to stop normal, everyday assistance programs just because they want to discriminate against people's religion. It is long overdue . . . that we correct the decisions that the U.S. Supreme Court has heaped upon us.

The Separation of Church and State

I think it is important that we look at a particular term that is often used by people in this discussion. I hear people say, well, what does this mean about separation of church and State? I understand the questions. But I also worry when people pay more attention to a catch phrase than to what are the words of the U.S. Constitution. Because that phrase, "separation of church and State," although it has some use, is not found in the Constitution of the United States of America. No matter how many people try to claim that it is, all you have to do is pick up a copy of the Constitution and read it.

What does it say about religion? "Congress shall make no law respecting an establishment of religion or prohibiting the free exercise thereof." That phrase, "separation of church and State," is not found in the Constitution.

So the religious freedom amendment does not violate the concept of separation of church and State in the proper sense of that term, but unfortunately . . . people who are intolerant of other people's religions have distorted the proper meaning of that phrase. In the process, they have persuaded our courts to distort the first amendment. . . .

The government keeps expanding. . . . Whether you are

talking about schools or roads or if you are talking about drug counseling programs, if you are talking about trade, if you are talking about the price of apples and eggs and butter, the government is involved. When you have a constantly growing government, if you put in place a mistaken notion of separation of church and State and make an improper use of that term, then as government gets bigger, you are saying that religion has to leave the room.

Discrimination Against Religion

Over the past thirty years there has been an alarming separation of the people of this country from the longstanding religious heritage that had been woven into the fabric of our history. Ironically, the founding fathers, who had the tyranny of a national religion fresh on their minds, probably would never have envisioned a time in history like today, when religious expression and exercise of any kind in public places is shunned so adamantly by government. They were running from a government too involved in religion. Today, we now have a government that discriminates against religion!

With the succession of cases upholding the "wall of separation" between church and state, the Supreme Court, step by step, in interpreting the "establishment" and "free exercise" clauses of the First Amendment moved us to the point where there is now more constitutional protection for nude art than there is for public religious expression.

That is why I have joined with Mr. Istook of Oklahoma in support of the Religious Freedom Amendment.

Sanford Bishop, testimony before the House of Representatives Committee on the Judiciary, July 22, 1997.

When government comes in the door, religion must exit. So as government keeps growing, religion and its place in our lives has to shrink. That is not what the Founding Fathers intended. That is not what that phrase was intended to mean.

I want to share with members what the phrase properly means. This is not according to Ernest Istook; this is according to the Chief Justice of the United States Supreme Court, William Rehnquist. Justice Rehnquist is not one of those who has been trying to push religion and religious expression out of the public square. But Justice Rehnquist has dissented from what the court has done in so many ways.

Justice Rehnquist wrote an official dissent, and this was in the case of *Wallace v. Jaffree* in 1985. He wrote that the wrongful focus on the term separation of church and State has caused . . . "a mischievous diversion of judges from the actual intentions of the drafters of the Bill of Rights. The wall of separation between church and State is a metaphor based on bad history, a metaphor which has proved useless as a guide to judging. It should be frankly and explicitly abandoned." Those are the words of the Chief Justice of the U.S. Supreme Court.

Because people, instead of talking about the Constitution and our rights under the Constitution, have sought to persuade people that instead you just talk about this phrase, "separation of church and State."

The religious freedom amendment does not abandon the notion of separation of church and State. It just corrects it to the proper meaning. . . . Chief Justice Rehnquist wrote about the actual intent of the first amendment, . . . and I quote his words again, "The evil to be aimed at, so far as its drafters were concerned, appears to have been the establishment of a national church and perhaps the preference of one religious sect over another, but it was definitely not concerned about whether the government might aid all religions evenhandedly."

So the religious freedom amendment follows the correct interpretation and meaning. We do not establish any sort of official religion. We are not going to have a national church in the USA. But that does not mean that we cannot have evenhanded treatment of different religions, of all religions rather than suppressing them, rather than having this current, horrible standard that says you go into a classroom and if a child wants to pray, you silence them. . . .

Referring to God

If we look at the preamble of the religious freedom amendment, to secure the people's right to acknowledge God according to the dictates of conscience, is that not what we want? Is that not the freedom we want? We can acknowledge God according to what our conscience tells us ought to be the manner of doing so.

I hear some critics say, oh, my goodness, we cannot refer to God in the Constitution of the United States of America. What do we think the Founding Fathers did and the Declaration of Independence when they talked about a due regard for nature's God, when they said in the Declaration of Independence that we hold these truths to be self-evident, that all men are created equal, that they are endowed by their creator with certain inalienable rights, and that among these rights are life, liberty, and the pursuit of happiness, that to secure these rights, governments are instituted among men? Now, is that not something? The Founding Fathers said our rights do not come from government, they come from God, from our Creator, and the purpose of government, the whole reason for setting up government is to secure the rights given to us by God.

Now, to some people today perhaps that appears a strange notion, and so when we say let us put in the Constitution that people have a right to acknowledge God according to the dictates of conscience, they seem to think it is something strange. But I have looked through the constitutions of all 50 States. I ask my colleagues if they know that every one of our 50 States in their State constitutions refer to God. They do.

We can look at any State. . . . California's constitution includes the words that they are grateful to Almighty God for our freedom. . . . Arizona, in its constitution it says, grateful to Almighty God for our liberties. Idaho, grateful to Almighty God for our freedom. Kansas, grateful to Almighty God for our civic and religious privileges.

Maine, oh, listen to this in Maine: Acknowledging with grateful hearts the goodness of the sovereign ruler of the universe in affording us an opportunity so favorable to the design, and imploring God's aid and direction in its accomplishments. That is in a state constitution in Maine. Connecticut says that it acknowledges with gratitude the good providence of God. Indiana, grateful to Almighty God for the free exercise of the right to choose our own government. Nebraska, grateful to Almighty God for our freedom. Michigan, grateful to Almighty God for the blessings of freedom. New York, grateful to Almighty God for our freedom. . . .

In this age when so many people are trying to suppress religious expression in everyday life, is it not overdue that we make it clear in the national Constitution of the United States of America that people should be secure in their right to acknowledge God according to the dictates of conscience? . . .

The people that did so much to establish this Nation and the States and to establish and then to preserve our freedom and our liberty, they recognized that it is because of God Almighty that we have been able to do these things. Yet . . . it is sad that so many people want to wipe it out. They say, well, look, if we want to express something about religion, do it in the privacy of your own home, do it only at church.

But . . . if our constitutional rights only exist when we are in private and we cannot proclaim them in public, are they really a right anymore? If we were told we have a right of free speech, but not in public, we would have the media so up in arms about it. . . .

The American Experiment

If I could close and just share a thought expressed recently, just about 3 months ago by Pope John Paul II, concerned with religious freedom in the United States of America, when he received the new American ambassador to the Vatican just in December. He said this:

> It would truly be a sad thing if the religious and moral convictions upon which the American experiment was founded could now somehow be considered a danger to free society, such that those who would bring these convictions to bear upon your Nation's public life would be denied a voice in debating and resolving issues of public policy. The original separation of church and State in the United States was certainly not an effort to ban all religious convictions from the public sphere, a kind of banishment of God from civil society.

Those were the words of Pope John Paul II just in December 1997, expressing concern about religious freedom being stripped away in America.

The religious freedom amendment will correct that.

| *"That we would now begin seriously considering retreating from our national commitment to the separation of church and state is indeed lamentable."*

The U.S. Constitution Already Protects Religious Liberty

Derek H. Davis

Derek H. Davis is director of the J.M. Dawson Institute of Church/State Studies at Baylor University, Waco, Texas. He also edits the *Journal of Church and State*. In the following viewpoint, taken from testimony before Congress, Davis argues against a proposed constitutional amendment that would permit organized prayer and other religious practices on public property and prohibit any government discrimination based on religion. Davis contends that such an amendment would jeopardize the separation of church and state, which he believes is integral to the welfare of both religion and government in America. The amendment would also threaten the religious freedoms guaranteed by the First Amendment by radically altering its scope and meaning, he concludes.

As you read, consider the following questions:

1. What are the two basic aims of the proposed constitutional amendment discussed by Davis?
2. How might public prayer trivialize religion, according to the author?
3. What idea from ancient and medieval times is being reflected in the proposed constitutional amendment that Davis is opposing?

Reprinted from Derek H. Davis's statement before the U.S. House of Representatives Committee on the Judiciary, Subcommittee on the Constitution, on H.J. Res. 78, July 22, 1997.

To begin with, the proposed amendment is considerably more far-reaching in its effects than most Americans realize, and if passed and ratified by the states, would overturn more than two centuries of settled church-state theory and practice in the United States. I share the concerns of those who support the amendment concerning the moral slide in America, the antidote to which, at least in part, is supposedly this amendment, but this amendment is no answer, and in my view its passage will only worsen the situation. This proposal performs radical surgery on the First Amendment, a surgery from which I fear many of the freedoms now guaranteed by the First Amendment might never recover.

Two Basic Aims

The proposed amendment has two basic aims. The first is to address the right of Americans to engage in prayer and other religious acts on public property. Of course the obvious but unstated goal here is to increase religious activity in the public schools. But school children already have the right to pray silently at any time, to gather to pray and study before or after school or at lunchtime, to wear clothing with religious symbols or messages, to distribute religious literature provided the educational process is not disrupted, and, under the Equal Access Act, to form prayer and Bible study groups in most middle and high schools. So what is really intended by the proposed amendment? Frankly, it is not clear. The wording is very ambiguous. It attempts to secure the "people's" right to pray and acknowledge their religious beliefs on public property. But who are the "people"? This could refer to the free exercise rights of private citizens in public forums, but it is subject to a broader interpretation. The "people" could refer to the people acting through their government representatives. If so, then local school boards would have the right to institute teacher-led prayers, meaning that the amendment would effectively overrule the *Engel*, *Schempp*, and *Wiseman* decisions which limit classroom and commencement prayer. It would also mean that local and state governments, acting for the people, could declare Texas to be a Baptist state, Utah a Mormon state, and the U.S. a Christian nation. A narrower construction would require judges to rule in favor of students whose "private" religious activities are sometimes limited by the Establishment Clause under current rulings. For example, courts are divided over the question of whether a high school senior class should be permitted to hold an election to designate one of its members to lead a commencement prayer. Some courts say this is protected by the Free Exercise Clause; others say the practice violates the Establishment Clause because the school is still in charge of the ceremony, is making facilities available, is giving tacit endorsement of the religious activity, etc. The courts that have frowned on the practice have all made the point that submitting the matter to majority vote is disrespectful of religious minorities, and amounts to a circumvention of the spirit of the Bill of Rights. My own view is that we should leave such complex matters in the hands of the courts, giving them the time and latitude to resolve such issues rather than prematurely preempting them through a constitutional amendment.

Even under a narrow construction, children would still be allowed to offer classroom prayers, probably on a rotating basis, to whomever they want—to God, to Allah, to the Rev. Sun Yung Moon, to Satan, to Sofia, or to any other conceivable deity. While the amendment champions this arrangement as "religious liberty," it would, I believe, actually devalue religion, even trivialize religion, particularly in the minds of young children. Whatever may be said about the right of each person within American society to express his or her belief through public prayer, one should question whether we want to convey the message that every religious and philosophical belief is on equal par with all others.

The second purpose of the amendment is to provide that government shall not "discriminate against religion or deny equal access to a benefit on account of religion." This provision alone turns current First Amendment jurisprudence on its ear. State and federal government would be required to fund religion just as they now fund secular activities. This makes the so-called "accommodation" approach to Establishment Clause interpretation a reality. Government may fund religion, as long as it does so nondiscriminatorily. All 2000 or so religious groups in America will have their hand out for their share of benefits. Even if we could afford it, the effects would be disastrous to religion in several basic ways. First, religious groups would lose their autonomy from government, and a new era of government regulation would follow made necessary by churches' use of government dollars. Second, fearful of the loss of benefits, churches would, over time, resign their "prophetic role" in society; churches with their hand out will be far less bold in calling government to account, far less willing to challenge and critique questionable government policies. Third, government could never equally fund all religions even if it wanted to. Religions with less political clout will be denied their share of the pie. It will be a "free for all," hardly what should characterize religion in America. Moreover, under this amendment citizens would be required through their taxes to support and advance other persons' religious beliefs, even those religions the taxpayer finds offensive. Jefferson, Madison, and a host of other founders, if possible, would rise from their graves in protest.

Religious Minorities

What is most offensive to me about this amendment is the effect it would have on religious minorities. Because, at least according to a recent poll by Goldhaber Research Associates, 83.8 percent of American religion is still Christian, 83.8 percent of the benefits could (and probably would) go to Christian churches and organizations. This is, if I may be so critical of many of my fellow Christian evangelicals who support the idea, a "back-door" method of "claiming the culture for Christ," as one of the amendment's supporters put it. It is never God's work to ride the back of government to advance a religious message. If Christianity cannot be formally established in the U.S., this amendment achieves the next best thing: an informal establishment made possible by the flood of benefits flowing to Christian groups. Religious minorities would be crushed under the weight of Christian majoritarianism, which is precisely why you will struggle to find informed members of religious minorities who favor this amendment. What Madison called in *Federalist* #10 "the superior force of an interested and overbearing majority," would surely have found a way to prevail under this amendment. If we wish to drive a huge wedge between non-Christians and their government, a good way to do it would be to pass this amendment.

An Unnecessary Amendment

While I agree with the sponsors of the [Religious Freedom] Amendment that we must foster respect for religion, I have grave reservations about this legislation and the impact it would have on the lives of many Americans.

First, this amendment is not necessary. If it were, I would be the first to support it. However, in thirty years of teaching and researching religious issues, I have never encountered an obstacle that prevented me from using my First Amendment right to talk about God, write about God, or express my faith. Furthermore, the people I represent, the many students that I have had the pleasure of teaching, and the religious communities that I have worked with throughout my career do not want this amendment. Why? Because they already enjoy the protection that the First Amendment has guaranteed them for over 200 years.

Second, the Istook Amendment would endanger the religious freedoms that have protected my work and my faith for most of my life. While I deeply respect my colleagues' desire to ensure religious freedom, this amendment has the potential to do just the opposite. If passed, the amendment could lead to government endorsement of particular religions at the expense of others.

Walter Capps, testimony before the House of Representatives Committee on the Judiciary, July 22, 1997.

In sum, this amendment would open up practices we thought we were putting behind us two hundred years ago when our Constitution and Bill of Rights were adopted. It would represent a return to ancient and medieval thinking where religion and government were merged and thought to be indistinguishable in their goals. Those societies, including Greece, the Roman Empire, and Medieval Europe, believed that the advancement of religion by *government* was essential to social solidarity and the happiness of the people. The modern idea of the separation of church and state resulted from the religious pluralism that was an outgrowth of the Reformation, and the accompanying recognition that religion is perhaps more a matter of private conscience than public concern. The atrocities of the Middle Ages and the Reformation in which hundreds of thousands died in Inquisitions, pogroms, witch-hunts, and religious wars, were thought to be the result of government having too much authority in matters of religion. In the U.S., the First Amendment's proscription against religious establishments and its allowance for the free exercise of religion virtually guaranteed a religiously pluralistic society—and the inability of any form of faith to achieve dominance. Passage of the proposed amendment would create a whole new framework of fusion of religion and government—in essence, a reversal of the separation that occurred at the founding and a return to the classical and medieval type polity in which government actively promoted religion as the glue of the social order. That we would now begin seriously considering retreating from our national commitment to the separation of church and state is indeed lamentable. The separation idea, as a grand experiment in human history, is still in a state of infancy. It is to be expected that problems within the separation framework will arise from time to time. The solution is not to rewrite the First Amendment, but to give our courts and legislatures the time and space to work out problems as they arise. And if the courts' decisions are necessarily complex at times, we must invest more time in educating the American people and in educating our educators, so that they will not make the grave mistake of denying to a child the right to pray at lunch, read her bible on the bus, or share her faith during recess, all of which are the unfortunate product of notions that have never been countenanced by the law.

I urge you to work for the defeat of the proposed amendment. Its supporters seem genuine in their motives to expand religious liberty in our great nation, but this amendment, like so many similar attempts by government leaders to aid religion throughout Western history, would actually do real damage to religious persons and religious institutions.

*"Those who . . . insist that it is inappropriate
to bear any costs for religious accommodation
are guilty of . . . overarching secularism."*

Special Legal Protections
Are Necessary to Ensure
Religious Freedom

Marc D. Stern

In 1993 Congress passed the Religious Freedom Restoration
Act (RFRA). RFRA established that general state and federal
laws could not impose "substantial" burdens on religious exercise unless there was a "compelling" state interest. In
1997, however, the Supreme Court ruled that Congress had
exceeded its constitutional authority in passing this law. The
following viewpoint is taken from testimony given by Marc
D. Stern before Congress in hearings following the Supreme
Court's 1997 ruling. Stern is a lawyer with the American
Jewish Congress. He argues that RFRA served as a useful
lever to ensure that public officials, teachers, and others respected the rights of religious practitioners. Without RFRA
or similar legislation, Stern concludes that religious liberties
in America are threatened.

As you read, consider the following questions:
1. How does Stern characterize litigants in religious liberty
   cases?
2. What examples of government repression of religious
   freedom does the author describe?
3. What comparison does Stern make between efforts to
   protect religious liberty and libel law?

Excerpted from Marc D. Stern's testimony before the U.S. House of Representatives
Committee on the Judiciary, Subcommittee on the Constitution, on behalf of the
American Jewish Congress, March 26, 1998.

On behalf of the American Jewish Congress, I want to thank you for this opportunity to describe the ways in which the demise of the compelling interest test of *Sherbert v. Verner* and *Wisconsin v. Yoder*, and the Supreme Court's invalidation of the Religious Freedom Restoration Act as it applied to the states and local governments, have impacted on my practice as a specialist in religious liberty.

[Editor's note: In *Sherbert v. Verner* in 1963, the Supreme Court ruled that a person who for religious reasons refused a job requiring her to work on Saturday was still entitled to state unemployment benefits. In *Wisconsin v. Yoder* in 1972, the Supreme Court ruled that states do not have the unlimited right to mandate school attendance to age 16 if that conflicted with a religious group's beliefs. With these and other rulings, the Court prohibited any government restrictions on religious expression unless the government could prove a compelling interest was at stake and no alternative existed to imposing such limits. It was this strict constitutional test that the Supreme Court abandoned in its 1990 case of *Department of Employment Services v. Smith*, and which Congress was attempting to restore with the passage of RFRA in 1993.]

At the outset, I would note that most of the people who consult with me are without question sincere in their assertion of a conflict between religious belief and governmental action. To be sure, there are some few persons who used Sherbert-Yoder or RFRA either in pursuit of a non-religious objection or merely to harass government officials. (The latter category is limited only to a small percentage of prison suits.) These individuals abusing the law are decidedly the minority. People simply do not undertake the burden of dissent from neutral laws without good reason. . . .

I would tell you that in now over twenty years of practice in this area I have found it necessary to litigate only in a handful of cases. This, even though I have been involved in literally hundreds of clashes between faith and law over the years. Most who find themselves caught between government regulation and religious belief are not interested in litigation or a public vindication of their principles or publicity. They are not interested in a defeat for the secular values embodied in the challenged government action, or in defeating the forces of secularism or evil. They simply want to be allowed to put their faith into practice with a minimum of fuss or burden to themselves or others. They are prepared to do what they can to accommodate the government so long as their religious concerns are taken seriously and accommodated if possible.

A Useful Mechanism

Not every claim made in the name of religious liberty can or should be granted. Some claims are simply beyond the power of a civilized society to grant. Others would do too much harm to the social fabric. But in my experience, a majority of cases lend themselves to creative solutions, to compromises, to different ways of achieving the same governmental end, but in a manner that is compatible with religious practice. And some forms of government activity are just not important enough to justify imposing on religious faith. What is needed is a mechanism to force negotiations, to compel public officials to move beyond a mentality of "this is the way we do things—we don't make exceptions," and to force a recognition in these days of omnipresent government that not everything government regulates or undertakes is equally weighty or that there is only one way to do things. When a mechanism is available to force a second look (and, unfortunately, that mechanism sometimes must be the big, thick and clumsy club of litigation) it is often possible to work out compromises acceptable to both sides, compromises that value and preserve as far as possible the legitimate interests of all concerned. Under the current state of the law, however, that mechanism or club is largely missing. There is nothing with which the religious believer can force the government to try something different, or reconsider its demand for total compliance even where that something different comes at little or no cost to the government, or even where it may be better than what government demands. Certainly nothing in federal law can be used to that purpose. It is that lacunae which I hope this committee will find a creative way of addressing within the confines of federal power as determined by the Supreme Court.

I do not wish to be misunderstood as suggesting that given the overruling of *Sherbert* and *Yoder* religious persecution is now common in the United States. It is not. Nor can I contend that since Boerne there are numerous horror stories with which to illustrate the urgent necessity of a response.

Changes in the law rarely have such an immediate impact. There are changes which I have already felt. There will be many more as government officials from legislators on down realize that they no longer need to accommodate religion. Rules that have allowed for religion to be accommodated—from statutory exemptions to the priest-penitent privilege to the ban on official resolution of intra-church disputes—will be reexamined, and in many cases, discarded. Religious persecution and inquisitions will not take their place, but we will have relegated religious freedom to a value less weighty than any other value enshrined in law. . . .

Examples of Religious Accommodation

An example. . . . The director of an Immigration and Naturalization Service [INS] detention facility refused to provide detainees—some of whom were probably seeking asylum from religious persecution—pork-free diets. His attitude was: this is the diet, if you do not want to eat it, starve. Because the President has ordered federal officials to comply with RFRA, when threatened with a lawsuit, the manager agreed to provide a pork-free diet. It was the availability of a club which brought this matter to a speedy conclusion. But if these detainees were held in a state or local facility under contract with the INS—as is the case in my home state of New Jersey—the detainees would have now no recourse under federal law. It is surely not plain why federal dollars should not carry with them the same obligation of religious accommodation on a local government contractor that the federal government imposes on itself. Whether an INS detainee is able to observe his faith in detention should not depend on whether he or she is incarcerated in a federal or local facility. As the law stands now, it does.

The impact of the absence of a lever with which to force thought of workable alternatives cannot be underestimated. Just weeks before the [1990] decision in *Employment Division v. Smith*, I received a call from a Jewish community in South Carolina. It seems that a school district had a rule barring the wearing of hats in school. The rule was applied to a Jewish boy who wished to wear a yarmulke in school as Orthodox Jewish practice requires. I told the community to inform the school board that if they did not waive the rule, I would sue it within 24 hours. Not surprisingly, the school board rethought application of its rule, and accommodated its student. I could not do that today. Indeed, it is doubtful that if I were to litigate that case, whether I would get beyond a motion to dismiss for failure to state a claim.

Reprinted by permission of Chuck Asay and Creators Syndicate.

Rules against headgear are generally defended as an anti-gang measure. I am unaware of any gang that has adopted the yarmulke as its signature. What the adoption of rules like that of this South Carolina district tells us is that the scope of religious liberty is today determined by the least law abiding elements of society, that the most naive and otherworldly believer may have his or her liberty restricted because some lawbreaker might do something similar. The test of RFRA was well adapted to ferret out those cases where the state's interest was truly important and where it was ephemeral, and more importantly, where the state's interest could be accomplished in some other way. Today, there is no such check.

Autopsies and Religious Belief

Some three years ago [in 1995], a friend of mine was killed on a commuter train when another train coming in the opposite direction ran a red signal. My friend was sitting at the point of impact. No one in the whole state doubted the cause of death. The coroner insisted upon an autopsy as the condition for certifying the cause of death. The family of the deceased objected on religious grounds to the performance of an autopsy. The coroner was adamant. I asked the coroner if either a CAT scan or an MRI would be acceptable. I was told that the coroner would not accept either alternative. RFRA was in force and a lawsuit was threatened. The State Attorney General advised the coroner that the lawsuit could not be won. A CAT scan showed the cause of death was a severed spinal cord. Here again, the ability to force a second look, to force a consideration of alternatives, led to a result which was acceptable to both sides, which resulted in the preservation of the reliability of death certificates and yet respected the religious beliefs of a grieving family. But nothing in federal law now forces that second look.

Just recently, I was involved in another case involving the same coroner. But because I had no federal right to force the use of—indeed, even the consideration of—alternatives, I was forced to rely on a state law which provides relatively little flexibility and does not explicitly require the consideration of alternatives. Ultimately, the coroner and I worked out an acceptable arrangement, only because this coroner (for whom I have much respect) is respectful of the feelings of believers. But this is personal to her and her office. Not every medical examiner takes matters of faith into account.

So when I recently wrote on the subject of autopsies and the law for a pastoral journal for Orthodox rabbis, I was obligated to tell them that in dealing with coroners they must recognize, as I am certain that many do not, that they cannot assume that because autopsies raise religious difficulties for Orthodox Jews, that the freedom of religion that they take for granted has any legal force in any concrete dispute over an autopsy, no matter how gratuitous. (Some state statutes give medical examiners virtually unfettered authority to require an autopsy.) Thus, I wrote, they should begin by assuming that the decision whether to conduct an autopsy lies totally within the discretion of medical examiners. Their approach, I suggested, should be one of the supplicant seeking a favor, not a citizen demanding respect for a fundamental right. I want to repeat that I do not contend that every religious claim must be accepted. Of course, only sincerely religious claims need be considered. As I noted at the outset, in some cases the costs of accommodations are simply too high to tolerate. Sometimes truly crucial interests are at stake. In others it will be impossible to devise a workable alternative. It does not follow that religious practice must yield to any governmental interest no matter how slight. And we need to view with some skepticism the persistent and universal response of "it is too expensive, too dangerous, too disruptive" to accommodate religious practice. Two cases, one of which I helped litigate many years ago, further illustrate the point.

Other Cases

Ohio requires slow moving vehicles to be marked with orange reflective tape. The Amish objected to the color of the tape but not to reflective tape of a more modest color, such as white. The state insisted on orange. The trial testimony demonstrated that the Amish's proposed alternative was more visible than the state-mandated orange. That is, it was safer. Because of RFRA, the Amish prevailed. They would not even be allowed to introduce that evidence today, let alone prevail on it.

The Illinois Athletic Association required ball players to play bare-headed. Now this is a classic facially neutral rule, and it was generally applicable. It is also the case that it would never be adopted in a league composed of Orthodox boys (or perhaps Moslem women), so that the claim of neutrality is less than it seems. In any event, the league defended its rule on grounds of safety concerns. It argued that if players wore hats, the hats might fall off and other players could trip over them. It's possible, but surely not common among young Orthodox boys (which I used to be) that a yarmulke would fall off, and someone else would trip and break a bone or otherwise be injured. When an Orthodox school sought to play in the league and have its students wear yarmulkes it was told no. Safety was invoked. (The league actually commissioned a study on whether yarmulkes made of different materials—cotton, wool, velvet, etc.—would lessen the likelihood of injury. That document is one of the proudest possessions of my organization). But, said the schools, our boys can attach their yarmulkes to their hair with clips so they will not fall off. Under Sherbert-Yoder, the Seventh Circuit held that alternative had to be explored. And indeed it was on those terms that the case ultimately settled, and that settlement remains in effect, as far as I can tell, without any problem.

Under current [1998] law, the case does not begin—the rule was facially neutral, and it was reasonable. End of case. But why should that be in a society which values religious diversity and relies on individual initiative? And if we require governmental bodies which receive federal funds to accommodate the handicapped in their athletic departments, and if we require them to see to it that boys and girls have an equal opportunity to participate in sports, why should we not require recipients of federal funds to give serious and weighty consideration to religious practices?

These are cases in which the costs of accommodation were small or nil. Indeed, in the Amish case it may well be that the process of exploring accommodations pointed to a better result for all.

The Costs of Religious Liberty

Religious liberty does not have to be cost free to be worthy of protection. If religious liberty means only that practitioners may practice what others may do it is not a value of any importance in our society. Presumably, every law, every ordinance, every governmental action furthers some public purpose. Presumably, too, the public as a whole is better off for the enforcement of these rules than their non-enforcement. But it is hardly a secret that sometimes larger values, sometimes abstract in the form of what we call rights, take precedence over more narrowly focused and more immediately beneficial policies. This is assuredly true when the question is not the general enforceability of the rule, but whether total compliance is necessary to further the government's interests.

Religious Freedom Under Siege

The religious freedom of Americans is currently under a quiet but substantial siege. While freedom of conscience— the ability to believe what you want—is unquestioned, the ability to act freely on beliefs can be severely hampered. When religious activity runs up against prized American secular interests, religion often loses. This sad truth is most evident in two contexts. . . .

The first context in which religious exercise is under fire is when it runs up against a seemingly neutral law or regulation. In our highly regulated society, hardly any activity can be undertaken without implicating some public policy concern. A religious community seeking to erect or expand a synagogue, church or mosque must contend with local zoning regulations. A public school student wishing to wear religious garb must contend with the school district's dress code requirements. . . .

The second context in which religious commitment is at odds with a prime American interest is when it runs up against capitalism. On a regular basis, American workers are asked to make the cruel choice between observing their faith and keeping a job. In some workplaces, Muslim women are told to remove their head-scarves, Orthodox Jews are pressed to work on Friday night and Christians are told to punch in on Christmas.

Nathan J. Diament, "Religion in the workplace: We don't respect faith when it's acted on," *The Washington Times*, September 6, 1999, p. A19.

Perhaps the most obvious example is the law of libel after *New York Times v. Sullivan*. [Editor's note: In this 1964 case, the Supreme Court ruled that a newspaper could not be sued and punished for publishing untrue statements about a public official unless it could be proved that the newspaper acted with "actual malice" and knew its reporting was false or acted with reckless disregard for the truth.] I do not share the view that "words can never hurt me." False statements, even about people occupying places of prominence, can and do damage reputations. I surely do not need to tell veterans of the rough and tumble political process that the truth sometimes does not catch up to the slander and libels that accompany political life. Defamation lawsuits serve an important purpose in providing redress.

But the vindication of reputation comes at a price to self governance, in self censorship to avoid the costs of a defamation suit. That is a cost we have generally deemed too high a cost for the benefit conferred in the case of public figures, at least in the absence of malice. Individuals are denied redress not because what was said about him was true, or yet because her reputation suffered no damage, but because larger social interests demand that the individual bear some of the costs of living in a democratic society that depends on an informed electorate. One could multiply examples from other fields of constitutional law; indeed from public policy generally.

The same notion applies to religious liberty. Obviously, there are limits, as there are in other fields. An important limit in the area of accommodation is the constitutionally mandated ban on forcing others to participate in another's religious practice. An inmate has the right to practice her faith—subject to the institution's interest in security and good order, and subject to legitimate logistical concerns—but she does not have the right to practice her faith in a way that compels others to participate against their will. I cannot conceive off-hand of a right to inflict physical harm on an unwilling adult.

It does not follow that no costs are appropriate to impose on society generally, or even on individuals. A liberty is a legal claim that trumps other claims. Almost by definition it comes at a cost. Those who would insist that it is inappropriate to bear any costs for religious accommodation are guilty of what [Supreme Court] Justice Arthur Goldberg warned against in another regard—an overarching secularism, which is hostile to religion, not merely neutral.

"Religious liberty is a laudable legislative concern, but it can be furthered only by legislation that expands the liberties available to everybody."

Special Legal Protections Are Not the Best Way to Ensure Religious Freedom

Christopher L. Eisgruber and Lawrence G. Sager

Christopher L. Eisgruber and Lawrence G. Sager are law professors at the New York University School of Law. In the following viewpoint, they criticize the Religious Freedom Restoration Act (RFRA), a 1993 federal law that gave religious organizations and individuals special exemptions from federal and state statutes in cases where such laws interfered with religious practice. (RFRA has been substantially rendered moot by a 1997 Supreme Court ruling.) Eisgruber and Sager argue that granting special rights and exemptions on the basis of religion is a flawed way of ensuring religious liberty. Religious freedom can be best protected by expanding personal liberty and flexibility in law enforcement for everyone, religious or not, the authors conclude.

As you read, consider the following questions:
1. What were some of the ramifications of the RFRA, according to Eisgruber and Sager?
2. In what area do the authors differ from the Supreme Court in the ruling *Department of Employment Services v. Smith*?
3. What mistaken view concerning freedom of religion do Eisgruber and Sager seek to correct?

Reprinted, with permission, from "Special Exemptions," by Christopher L. Eisgruber and Lawrence G. Sager, *Liberty*, November/December 1998.

Imagine living in a quiet residential neighborhood when a nearby homeowner (call her Mrs. Campbell) starts running a soup kitchen from her garage. Some neighbors object, fearful that the soup kitchen will increase traffic and attract "undesirables" to the area. They persuade town officials to enforce their zoning ordinance and stop Mrs. Campbell.

Mrs. Campbell sues, seeking to exempt her charitable project from the zoning ordinance. At the hearing the judge says, "Now, Mrs. Campbell, I need to know whether you are running this soup kitchen because of your religious beliefs. If you are, then I'll permit you to go ahead. If you're not, I won't."

Surely the judge's question is an affront to religious liberty. Perhaps one can sympathize with Mrs. Campbell, and believe that charitable endeavors ought to enjoy special exemptions from zoning laws. Or perhaps one sympathizes with the unhappy neighbors, and believe that Mrs. Campbell ought to move her otherwise laudable project to a more suitable location. But either way her right to do good works and her right to use her property as she wishes ought not to depend upon her religious beliefs.

Consider the bizarre and uncomfortable questions that would arise in the colloquy between the judge and Mrs. Campbell. Suppose Mrs. Campbell has long felt it intolerable for people to go hungry as a matter of simple justice, but also felt that her religion counsels that people should aid the needy. Does it matter whether she has more than one reason for doing good works? Or suppose, while Mrs. Campbell's faith requires her to care for the needy, it recognizes that there are many forms such care can take. Or suppose that within her faith charitable acts are regarded as good but not requisite for leading a religious life. Does it matter just how specific and how demanding Mrs. Campbell's religion is? Does it matter whether Mrs. Campbell attends regular church services? Would she be religious in the right way if she were moved to a life of good works by what she called "Christian ethics," even if she had little or no interest in Christian theology? And suppose Mrs. Campbell shared responsibility for the soup kitchen with her husband, an avowed secular humanist. Would the kitchen be legally permissible on days that she ran it, but not on days when he alone was present?

The Misguided Religious Freedom Restoration Act

Is it preposterous to imagine—in a nation that loves liberty and especially prizes freedom of belief—that Mrs. Campbell could be called to account for her beliefs and commitments in this way? No. In fact, it has become fashionable for the government to make rights contingent on religious belief in just this manner, and thus to require judges to act like the judge in Mrs. Campbell's case. The paradigmatic example of this is the Religious Freedom Restoration Act (RFRA). As its name indicates, RFRA was enacted in the service of religious liberty. Yet it was a misguided attempt to achieve a laudable purpose.

Under RFRA some churches were able to duck zoning laws and operate soup kitchens in residential neighborhoods when everyone else was prohibited from the same. Some bankrupt religious debtors were able to circumvent bankruptcy laws and make charitable contributions when all other debtors were prevented from doing so. Some religious landlords claimed that they should be able to defy civil rights laws that prohibited everyone else from discriminating against unwed couples. It was even the case that some religious men who flouted child-support obligations were excused from contempt sanctions imposed upon other "deadbeat dads."

In *City of Boerne v. Flores*, the Supreme Court held that RFRA was unconstitutional, at least insofar as it purported to constrain state and local governments. But the era of RFRA has not necessarily passed. RFRA itself may continue to apply to federal legislation like the bankruptcy laws, since *Flores* focused on Congress's power to apply the act to state and local laws. Meanwhile, many states are considering statutes patterned upon RFRA, and some members of Congress are considering legislation that would reproduce the effects of RFRA but would try to circumvent *Flores*.

What explains RFRA's popularity? Its defenders point out that laws that are neutral on their face can nevertheless impair the ability of religious believers to practice their faith. That is true, and it's a problem of great concern. RFRA's supporters accordingly believe that this leaves Americans in a kind of Free Exercise dilemma. Special privileges to disobey otherwise valid and reasonable laws, reserved for the truly religious alone, may be awkward—but such privileges are the only way to accommodate the needs of religious believers.

A Better Way

There is, however, a better way to promote a strong version of free exercise. First, judges and legislators should take a generous view of personal liberty, not just for religious believers, but for all people. Second, when the government carves out special exceptions for the benefit of secular interests, it should be required to do the same for comparable religious interests. And finally, when the government imposes broad, generally applicable restrictions on conduct, it should show the same sensitivity to minority religious interests that it shows to mainstream religious and secular interests.

Start with the idea that the Constitution should be understood to guarantee a generous share of liberty for all people. It's easy to see how that liberty will benefit religious believers. For example, in the famous case of *West Virginia v. Barnette*, some schoolchildren refused to comply with a state law requiring them to salute the flag. They had religious grounds for their choice: they were Jehovah's Witnesses, and their faith forbade them from honoring any graven image. The Supreme Court upheld the children's right to opt out of the flag salute ceremony, but it did so without creating any special privilege for religious believers. The Court declared that the state simply had no power to compel anybody to salute the flag.

As a second example, consider one of the more appealing claims that arose under RFRA. Orthodox Jews have sought relief from zoning decisions that prohibited them from using their homes as *shteebles*—that is, from using them for small regular worship services. Orthodox Jews should have the right to conduct such services. They should have it, though, not as the result of any special privilege unique to religious believers, but because the Constitution protects the right of all people to invite friends, acquaintances, and neighbors to gather with them in their homes for peaceful purposes. One might even construe this right broadly enough to encompass Mrs. Campbell and her soup kitchen (and, of course, if Mrs. Campbell enjoys such a right, so too should any church operating in a residential neighborhood).

Victims of Religious Liberty Statutes

[A] factor that has prevented the states from blindly adopting . . . [statutes exempting religions from burdensome state and local laws] has been the slow awakening of those groups most harmed by these one-size-fits-all laws. The following need to be brought in the discussion if the right balance of power is to be achieved: likely victims of discrimination by religious landlords and employers, likely victims of child abuse and neglect at the hands of certain religious sects, likely victims of spousal abuse, pediatricians, child advocates, municipal and county governments, zoning boards, historical and cultural preservation groups, prisons, religious groups that are willing to admit that there is no religious interest in trumping every law, and the Agnostics and Atheists who cannot benefit from the special privileges religion receives from the law. When these groups are silent because they are uninformed, legislators labor under the delusion that anything they do for religion is good for society—and good for their next election. But when these interests are heard, the bills' legislative sponsors have taken a tempered approach.

Marci A. Hamilton, *American Atheist*, Autumn 1998.

Home schooling provides a third illustration. Religious parents may have special reasons for wishing to educate their children at home. They may, for example, want to protect their children from influences that might damage their faith. Or they may think it desirable to provide a pervasively religious learning experience of a kind that is, in their judgment, not available from any school in their area. Such parents should have the right to school their children at home. But it should be recognized that their religious interests are a specific version of a more widely shared interest—the interest that all parents have in providing the best possible education and upbringing for their children. And the constitutional right protecting them should be equally broad: it should respect the autonomy of all parents, not merely those who have religious motives for their decision.

Consider now the second prong of this approach to religious liberty, which demands that government not turn a blind eye to religious interests when it crafts exemptions for secular ones. A recent First Amendment case from Newark, New Jersey, nicely illustrates the point. Newark's police department requires that its officers be clean-shaven. Two Islamic policemen sought an exemption on religious grounds; their faith required that they wear beards. The police department refused to relax its rule, but a federal district court granted relief. The court pointed out the police department made an exception for police officers with sensitive skin, who would suffer a rash if forced to shave. Since the department was willing to accommodate the special interests of officers susceptible to skin rashes, it was obliged to be equally receptive to the religious interests of the Islamic officers.

The *Smith* Case

So far these recommendations have been quite consistent with the Supreme Court's current reading of the free exercise clause. The third suggestion makes a departure from the Court's free exercise doctrine. In *Department of Employment Services v. Smith*, the Court addressed a claim from practitioners of a Native American religion who sought exemption from an Oregon law. The Native American faith involved the ritual consumption of peyote. Oregon law prohibited the possession or use of peyote.

In *Smith* the Supreme Court distinguished sharply between laws such as Newark's police department regulation, which included exceptions, and laws such as the Oregon peyote regulation, which did not. The Court announced a broad per se rule to deal with any exemption claim directed at laws such as Oregon's: "The right of free exercise does not relieve an individual of the obligation to comply with a valid and neutral law of general applicability on the ground that the law proscribes (or prescribes) conduct that his religion prescribes (or proscribes)."

The Justices did not want the impossible task of deciding which religious people deserved what privileges in cases about zoning, bankruptcy, education, and virtually every other imaginable topic of legal regulation. The Court's unease is understandable. But it does not justify a stark distinction between laws that include exceptions and laws that do not.

For example, the Oregon law against peyote consumption may have looked like a clean, bright-line rule with no exceptions. Suppose, though, one stepped back and looks at the law in its larger context. Oregon had a host of laws dealing with drug abuse. Among these was a law permitting counties to prohibit alcohol consumption. That law, however, contained an interesting provision: it required dry counties to make exceptions for the benefit of religious faiths (notably, Christian faiths) that use alcohol in religious rituals. Thus Oregon's laws may have reflected a failure to show equal regard for the practices of minority religious believers. Just as Newark made special exceptions to benefit those with special health problems but not those with special religious needs, Oregon's controlled substance laws included exceptions for the benefit of mainstream faiths but not minority ones.

Though it's possible to offer good reasons that peyote and alcohol should be treated differently, the basic point is clear: neutral and generally applicable laws may reflect a failure by the government to show equal regard for minority religious interests. Insofar as the Court in *Smith* was insensitive to the problem, its free exercise doctrine is unsatisfactory.

RFRA was passed in reaction to *Smith*, and the most generous way to view the statute is as an effort to cure the insensitivity of the *Smith* decision toward the requirement of equal regard for the needs of all citizens, including members of minority religious faiths. So understood, the goal of RFRA was impartiality, not special privilege. But so understood, RFRA was doomed from the outset. It incorporated the toughest test known to constitutional law, "the compelling state interest test." To defeat an exemption claim, the government had to show either that its law imposed no "substantial burden" on religious practices, or that it had a "compelling interest" to justify the burden. In the law's eyes, few interests count as "compelling." As a result, whatever RFRA was aiming at, it produced a stark, inequitable privilege available only to those who were religious, and religious in the right way.

This claim is not mere conjecture or academic argument. In one area after another courts found that RFRA demanded that some religious persons be excused from obeying reasonable and evenhanded laws, while secular persons who were otherwise in exactly the same position and religious persons who were acting on the basis of secular motives—however lofty and altruistic their motives might be—were required to obey those laws.

Free Exercise of Religion

RFRA's defects were not merely the product of clumsy legislative drafting. They emanated from a profoundly mistaken view of what it means to be "strong on free exercise." That view supposes that religious exercise is free only if religious conduct is presumptively and uniquely immune from any form of government regulation—and hence only if religious believers are presumptively entitled to special exemptions not available to others.

Professor Michael McConnell, an exponent of this idea, says that constitutional law should aspire to match a "hypothetical world in which individuals make decisions on the basis of their own religious conscience, without the influence of government." Government should, of course, stay out of church affairs, and it should not manipulate people's religious beliefs. But government cannot help having an enormous influence on the activities of churches and religious individuals, just as it has an enormous impact on all groups and individuals within any modern society. Government provides the security, resources, and stability without which religious faith and activity would be resoundingly difficult, if not impossible, to pursue. It inculcates and enforces principles of morality—such as, for example, the principle that persons enjoy equal status regardless of their race, faith, or sex, or the principle that speech should be free—which are more congenial to some religions than others. And it doles out ownership rights without which it would be impossible even to conceptualize questions about whether Mrs. Campbell can use "her" house to run a soup kitchen, whether for religious reasons or any other reasons.

Churches and religious individuals live within a society

permeated by law. They cannot help benefiting from the existence of the legal regime that surrounds them; indeed, it would be deeply unjust to deny them any of the benefits that are available to everyone else. So too, churches and religious individuals must respect the boundaries set by reasonable, evenhanded rules that everyone else is required to obey. That is the inevitable price that accompanies the benefits of the rule of law. Any law drafted in service of a conception of Free Exercise that fails to accept this simple proposition is likely to do far more harm than good to religious believers and to religious liberty itself.

RFRA is a case in point. Far from reducing the impact of government upon religion, RFRA overtly manipulated religious belief. Imagine Mrs. Campbell's reaction when she learned, from the judge or her lawyer, that the fate of her soup kitchen depended upon whether her motives were religious and religious in just the right sort of way. She would have an obvious incentive not just to characterize her motives in the most favorable way but to reconceive them in order to justify her characterization of them. There is something deeply insidious about a law that puts well motivated persons in the position of giving skewed witness to their own beliefs, under penalty of denying them the license to pursue those beliefs.

RFRA's demise has sparked a new round of legislative activity, including the so-called Religious Liberty Protection Act. Unfortunately, this bill, like nearly all the statutes now percolating in Congress and in the legislatures of many states, repeat RFRA's central error: they invoke the "compelling state interest" test. That is a great misfortune. Religious liberty is a laudable legislative concern, but it can be furthered only by legislation that expands the liberties available to everybody, or legislation that seeks to ensure that all interests (religious and secular, mainstream and minority) are treated impartially. Until legislators are ready to leave the mistakes of RFRA behind them, the legislation they produce will be ill conceived, counterproductive, and unconstitutional.

"Doctors may believe in the healing power of prayer, but they do not believe that diabetic children should be deprived of insulin."

Parents Must Provide Necessary Medical Treatment for Children Regardless of Religious Belief

Rita Swan

Some religious groups, notably Christian Scientists, reject standard medical treatment in favor of prayer. Many states have laws that exempt parents from child abuse and neglect laws if the parents act out of religious faith; a few states include exemptions for criminal homicide or murder charges. In the following viewpoint, Rita Swan decries such legal exemptions and contends that state governments have the duty to ensure that sick children receive care regardless of their parents' religious beliefs. Swan is president of Children's Healthcare Is a Legal Duty (CHILD), an organization working to reduce religion-based medical neglect of children.

As you read, consider the following questions:
1. What personal circumstances led Swan to her position on religion-based medical neglect?
2. What was the origin of many of the state laws conferring religious exemptions to civil codes, according to the author?
3. What examples of suffering caused by medical neglect does Swan describe?

Excerpted from "The Children We Abandon: Medical Neglect on Religious Grounds," by Rita Swan, *American Atheist*, Autumn 1998. Reprinted with permission from the author.

My husband and I were reared as Christian Scientists. In 1977 we lost our only son, Matthew, because of relying on Christian Science instead of going to a doctor when he contracted meningitis. We left the church immediately after his death and today belong to the Methodist Church. We have become nationally known for our opposition to medical neglect of children on religious grounds and to laws offering a religious exemption from child healthcare requirements.

The April 1998 issue of *Pediatrics* has an article by pediatrician Seth Asser and me reviewing deaths of children after medical care was withheld on religious grounds. Of 172 US child fatalities between 1975 and 1995, we found that 140 were from conditions for which survival rates with medical care would have exceeded 90%. We believe that the majority of deaths due to religion-based medical neglect do not come to our attention.

More than twenty sects have caused deaths of children in the past two decades because of their opposition to medical care. Several are small fellowships that spring up around a charismatic leader, while others, such as the Church of the First Born, are 300 years old.

The Jehovah's Witnesses, with millions of members, are the largest denomination with a religious objection to medical care. Fortunately, today, their only objection is to blood transfusions.

The Christian Science church will not disclose membership figures, but we believe it has fewer than 100,000 members. It is the largest denomination that objects to virtually all forms of medical care.

It also does virtually all the lobbying for religious exemptions. The church maintains a salaried lobbyist in every state and can quickly organize hundreds of calls, letters, and visits with legislators. . . .

Religious Exemptions

Forty-eight states have religious exemptions from immunizations. Mississippi and West Virginia are the only states that require all children to be immunized without exception for religious belief. As you would expect, many outbreaks of vaccine-preventable disease have occurred in groups claiming the religious exemption. . . .

Perhaps even more damaging than the religious exemptions from preventive and diagnostic measures are laws that appear to allow parents to withhold medical care when the child is actually sick. Today [in 1998] 41 states have religious exemptions from child abuse and neglect charges in the civil code, and 31 have religious exemptions in the criminal code. Most of these laws came into state codes because of a tragically misguided federal policy in place between 1975 and 1983. During that time the federal government coerced states to enact religious exemptions in the civil code by making them an eligibility requirement for federal money. Simultaneous state-by-state lobbying by the Christian Science church got many exemptions extended into the criminal code.

The actual reach of the religious exemptions varies widely. It definitely would not be accurate to say that all these states allow parents to withhold lifesaving medical care from children. The laws reflect the contortions and ambiguities of model language provided by the Feds. Some of the exemptions provide absolute immunity to criminal charges for parents who withhold medical care on religious grounds, while other exemption laws probably protect only the right to pray for a healing. . . .

There are, however, six states that have a religious defense to a homicide or manslaughter charge: Oregon, West Virginia, Delaware, Ohio, Iowa, and Arkansas. . . .

Oregon has laws offering religious immunity from charges of first- and second-degree criminal mistreatment, nonsupport, first- and second-degree manslaughter, and murder by abuse. . . .

[Oregon statutes] give religious immunity to charges of murder by abuse and to first- and second-degree manslaughter with the following sentence: "It is an affirmative defense to a charge of violating . . . this section that the child or dependent person was under care or treatment solely by spiritual means pursuant to the religious beliefs or practices of the child or person or the parent or guardian of the child or person."

These laws grant complete immunity from all these criminal charges regardless of what the parent or guardian is doing to the child. Parents may be torturing, beating, or sexually molesting the child, and all they have to prove is that they provided the child with spiritual treatment because of their religious beliefs—and the charges of manslaughter, murder by abuse, criminal mistreatment, or nonsupport must be dismissed.

Religious immunity to the three homicide charges was passed in 1995 and 1997 with the support of the Oregon District Attorneys Association. . . .

[Editor's note: Oregon repealed some of its religious exemptions in 1999.]

What Doctors Think

Early in 1998 the American Academy of Pediatrics published a second policy statement calling for the repeal of religious exemption laws so that all children will have equal rights to medical care. The Christian Science church responded by calling the pediatricians out of step with the culture:

> The American Academy of Pediatrics' new policy seems out of sync with society's growing acknowledgment of the effectiveness of prayer. Harvard Medical School has instituted symposiums on spirituality and healing. A recent survey of 269 doctors indicates 99% believe in the healing power of prayer. . . The public knows effective alternatives to conventional medicines exist, and people have the right to make intelligent choices among those treatments for themselves and their families.
>
> Isn't it time to stop talking of children as "property" and allow them the right to be healed through the treatment their families have found most effective. . . ? Religious accommodation puts a brake on aggressive zeal that would want all children placed under one healthcare system—a monopoly that aborts freedom of choice. Christian Science and traditional medicine should exist amicably. Mutual respect for what both offer can make that possible.

To me, the fallacies in this line of argument are transparent. The church is not asking for the right to pray; it is asking for its methods to be a legal substitute for medical care. Ninety-nine percent of doctors may believe in the healing power of prayer, but they do not believe that diabetic children should be deprived of insulin. Effective alternatives do not exist for the standard medical treatments for all diseases. How broad is the experience of parents who think religious healing is the most effective treatment? How much information do they have on the disease their child has now? The Christian Science church believes that knowledge of disease causes disease. They seek exemptions for their children from studying about disease at school. Obtaining a medical diagnosis violates their theology. So how can they make "intelligent choices" among alternative and conventional treatments when they don't even know what disease their child has?

Are those who call for repeal of religious exemptions being narrow-minded? Requiring parents to bring sick children to a doctor does not outlaw prayer. Every doctor I've ever met is happy for his or her patients to be prayed for. It

---

What Religions Object to Medical Care of Children?

This is a partial list of churches whose members have let children die since 1980 because of their religious beliefs against medical care:

- Faith Assembly
- Followers of Christ
- Christian Science
- Church of the First Born
- Faith Tabernacle
- End Time Ministries
- The Believers' Fellowship
- Faith Temple Doctoral Church of Christ in God
- Church of God of the Union Assembly
- Church of God Chapel
- Jehovah's Witnesses (Their only objection today is to blood transfusions.)
- Jesus through Jon and Judy
- Christ Assembly
- Christ Miracle Healing Center
- Northeast Kingdom Community Church
- "No Name" fellowship
- The Source

Children's Healthcare Is a Legal Duty, "Frequently Asked Questions," www.childrenshealthcare.org/question/htm.

---

is instead the faith-healing sects that insist you cannot have both God and a doctor. . . .

Church-Care as Medical Care

The Christian Science church wants to be both a health-care system and a religion. It uses some of the terminology of medical science, calling its faith healers practitioners, its prayers treatments, and those for whom they pray their patients. The practitioners send bills for their prayers, and the church has persuaded some forty insurance companies to pay the bills for the prayers. Charges often range between $20 and $50 a day for a prayer. The practitioners are allowed to sign sick leave and disability statements even though they have no training in diagnosis and their theology holds that disease is unreal.

The church also has people called nurses, who are not state-licensed and do little that resembles medical nursing. The Christian Science nurses cannot take a pulse, use a fever thermometer, give oxygen, or even a back rub. They will not apply heat or use ice to relieve inflammation. They have no training in recognizing contagious diseases.

They do feed patients and wash them, but their primary function is to encourage them or their parents to believe that Christian Science is healing them. They read church literature and sing hymns to them. Both Medicare and Medicaid have paid for Christian Science nursing since 1965. . . .

The Human Cost

Christian Science nurses have been retained to attend sick children and have sat taking notes as the children suffered and died, but have not called for medical care nor recommended that the parents obtain it. Elizabeth Ashley King, a twelve-year-old who died of bone cancer in Phoenix, Arizona, was out of public school for seven months. The school knew she was a Christian Scientist, but allowed a home-study program to be set up for her. When the case was finally reported to Child Protection Services and she was examined by a doctor, the tumor on her leg was more than forty inches in circumference and her genitalia were partially rotted away from lying in her own excrement. Because the disease was by then terminal and because the girl herself said she wanted to stay with Christian Science, the state allowed her to be placed in one of those Christian Science nursing homes that receive Medicare and Medicaid money. This was done over the protest of her treating physician, who said she was experiencing one of the worst kinds of pain known to mankind.

She spent the last three weeks of her life in the nursing home. Of course, she received no sedatives because the Christian Science religion opposes drugs. The nursing home records show 71 calls made to the Christian Science practitioner in those three weeks for more prayer treatments for Ashley's pain. Indeed, that is the only thing the church's nurses will do about pain is call a Christian Science practitioner for prayer. One nurse reminded this little girl of the lateness of the hour and that other patients were sleeping. Another nurse wrote in her notes that the tumor disappeared one day.

This is the kind of care that Congress has taxpayers paying for.

In suburban Minneapolis, eleven-year-old Ian Lundman died of untreated diabetes. A Christian Science nurse sat by his bedside for over five hours while he lay in a diabetic coma. Her notes show that she observed his facial spasms, vomiting, eyes rolled back, labored breathing, and urination, but her concept of care was to give him drops of water through a straw, wash his body, and place a sandwich bag and washcloth around his scrotum. She was asked in court what kind of training she had received specific to the care of children. The only thing she could think of was that she had been taught to cut sandwiches in interesting shapes.

A wrongful death suit was brought by Ian's father, who was divorced from the boy's Christian Science mother and was not told his son was seriously ill. In 1993 a jury awarded him $14 million, later reduced by the courts to $1.5 million.

Mr. Lundman has yet [as of 1998] to collect a penny of the judgment. But the principle has been established that tort liability is possible against Christian Science nurses and faith healers.

How Many Children?

The novelist John Dos Passos said our only hope as a society lies in the fragile web of understanding of one person for the pain of another. Unfortunately, our society's ability to imagine the pain experienced by children is tenuous. Too many people in positions of power are willing for these children to be second-class citizens. For some it's a numbers game. Medical doctor Larry Dossey says they are too few in number to disturb his contention that "prayer is good medicine." But isn't our form of government supposed to protect individual rights? The religious exemption laws deprive one class of children of the rights and privileges enjoyed by others.

How many are too few? We have reported on 172 documented faith deaths of US children between 1975 and 1995. Our work was a catalyst for the Oregon media to uncover the Followers of Christ, a congregation near Portland that rejects medical care. *The Oregonian* reported on June 7 that 78 children have been buried since 1955 in the church cemetery. The most recent case was that of Bo Phillips, age eleven, who died in February of untreated diabetes.

For decades public officials have swept these deaths under the rug. The new Clackamas County prosecutor would like to act, but says she is unable to file criminal charges against the parents because of Oregon's religious immunity laws. We did not know of any of the Followers of Christ deaths when we did our research. We suspect that even today we only know about the tip of the iceberg.

*"Quite properly, America has long respected
the right of the family to make religious
decisions for children."*

Parents Who Withhold Children's Medical Treatment Because of Religious Beliefs Should Not Be Punished

Stephen L. Carter

In 1993 the father of a boy who had died while being cared for by Christian Science practitioners was awarded $1.5 million in a wrongful death suit. In the following viewpoint, Stephen L. Carter contends the case raises serious questions about religious liberty in America. He argues that parents should have the right to practice their religion, even if it means making choices concerning their children that many people would find irrational. Carter is a law professor at Yale University and the author of several books on religion in American life, including *The Culture of Disbelief* and *God's Name in Vain: The Rights and Wrongs of Religion in Politics*.

As you read, consider the following questions:

1. What did Thomas Jefferson say about religious freedom, according to Carter?
2. What compromise does Carter propose concerning children of religious parents?
3. What social message is being sent about prayer by the Supreme Court, according to the author?

When Thomas Jefferson described religious freedom as "the most inalienable and sacred of all human rights," he could not have imagined that the time would come when American citizens would be forced to pay ruinous damages for exercising it.

But that is the result of the Supreme Court's decision [in January 1996] not to review the case of *McKown v. Lundman*. The decision let stand a Minnesota Court of Appeals ruling upholding an award of $1.5 million to the father of 11-year-old Ian Lundman, who died in 1989 after his mother, stepfather and two Christian Science practitioners tried to use prayer to heal his diabetes.

The mother and stepfather are devout Christian Scientists, who, after Ian complained of stomach pains, began to pray for him, as their religion prescribes. Eventually, they enlisted the services of the practitioners, who assisted in the prayers. Despite these efforts, the boy slipped into a coma and died. When medical experts testified later in court that insulin would have saved the child, the judicial fate of the defendants was evidently sealed.

But should matters have been so simple? Never before have Christian Science practitioners been held liable for trying and failing to heal the sick. Christian Science is not some bizarre new cult. Nobody claims that the boy's family was malicious or irrational. They meant Ian no harm. Like parents everywhere, they made the best choices they could, relying on their religious faith to help guide them.

A Widespread Belief in Prayer

Before one rushes to say that anybody who relies on prayer to cure a serious medical condition deserves to be punished, one should look at the data. According to an ABC News/Gallup poll taken in December 1995, four out of five respondents believe that prayer can cure diseases. Nearly half say that they themselves have been healed by prayer.

Some medical experts may deride this overwhelming majority as kooky, but there is scarcely a religion in America whose followers do not pray for deliverance from illness. And a majority of states have statutes explicitly recognizing a parent's right to try to heal sick children through faith.

The death of any child is a tragedy—but it is not a greater tragedy because it occurs as devout family members pray rather than as noble physicians struggle. Although the matter was once in dispute, no one questions any longer the right of an adult to refuse, on religious grounds, standard medical treatment for an illness.

When a child rather than an adult is involved, the right legal question is not what the decision should be but who should have the power to make it. Quite properly, America has long respected the right of the family to make religious decisions for children—a freedom older than the Constitution and one that the document did nothing to disturb.

From time to time, we hear objections to this broad parental freedom. In 1972, for example, Supreme Court Justice William O. Douglas dissented from *Wisconsin v. Yoder*, which allowed the Old Order Amish to take their children out of school after the eighth grade in spite of compulsory-education laws.

The Justices accepted the Amish argument that mandated schooling for their young people might destroy the Amish way of life. Justice Douglas responded that the children rather than the parents should make the decision.

Like most parents, I would make a different decision than Ian Lundman's parents did. But a family's religious freedom should not be limited by what other families would do.

Without freedoms of the kind that Justice Douglas disparaged, religious communities whose values differ sharply from the mainstream might be unable to survive, for survival often depends on the ability to raise children in an atmosphere that celebrates rather than demeans the faith of the parents.

Our self-righteous certainty that we know all the answers might lead us to decide that religions whose values are too different from ours do not deserve to survive.

This claim was common in the early years of this century, when a number of state legislatures, moved by nativist sentiments, outlawed private schools as a way of eradicating what they considered "foreign" religions—principally Judaism and Roman Catholicism.

The Supreme Court put a stop to this mischief in 1925, when it ruled that parents have a constitutional right to make educational choices for their children. How sad that seven decades later, our supposedly conservative Court could not move itself to say something similar about medical care.

A Christian Scientist Defends Spiritual Healing

Though adults have the right to choose any method of healing, health care for children is different. The state has a responsibility to ensure the proper care of children. In this context, then, the crucial question is: On what basis can the state ensure that when religious healing practices are involved, the children in question are being cared for responsibly?

If Christian Science is taken as one standard against which the question of responsible spiritual healing practice is judged, its record should contribute to an appropriate conclusion. Spiritual treatment, as practiced by this denomination, has a documented history of effective healings that has been published in Christian Science periodicals for more than 100 years. Each one is verified, and a portion of these are healings of medically diagnosed disorders, some even deemed by conventional medicine as incurable. A partial list of diagnosed conditions healed by Christian Science treatment include cancer, pneumonia, tuberculosis, kidney disorders, broken bones, meningitis, appendicitis, rheumatic fever, glaucoma, epilepsy, and birth defects. A significant percentage of these have involved children.

In view of the literally tens of thousands of verified healings accomplished via this treatment method, it is understandable that up to four, and now five, generations of stable, well-cared-for families have relied exclusively on Christian Science for their health-care needs.

M. Victor Westberg, *Liberty*, May/June 1998.

One might object that when the life of a child is at stake, the state's interest in intervening is unusually strong. I would agree, as I suspect most Americans would, so long as the state is able to intervene in a way that does not actually discourage the parents from following the teachings of their faith.

A Compromise

Under one compromise that several states have adopted, Christian Science practitioners are required to inform state medical authorities when they begin treating a child. This gives the state the chance to intervene and (as has happened in many cases) make medical decisions against the wishes of the parents.

Should the state use this power wisely and sparingly, the lives of some children will probably be saved, but no parents would be punished for religious devotion.

Like all compromises, this one offers less than total victory to each side. Like all good compromises, it preserves the essence of each side's position.

What the Minnesota courts did instead—award sufficient damages to drive the family into bankruptcy—was a sufficient affront to religious freedom that groups like the moderate Baptist Joint Committee and the National Association of Evangelicals urged the Supreme Court to take up the case.

By refusing to hear the family's appeal, the Justices have left the door open to all sorts of mischief. Within days after the Court's decision, newspapers ran articles about a 4-year-old Seattle boy whose mother is sending him off to live with Buddhist monks in Nepal because she and the monks believe that the boy is the reincarnation of a famous and respected lama.

If, upon reaching adulthood, the boy decides that he is not the lama after all, if he decides that his life has been ruined, could he sue his mother for exercising her faith? The answer, at least in Minnesota, is evidently yes.

By refusing to intervene in *McKown v. Lundman*, the Supreme Court has reinforced a societal message that has grown depressingly common: It is perfectly O.K. to believe in the power of prayer, so long as one does not believe in it so sincerely that one actually expects it to work—a peculiar fate indeed for our "most inalienable" right.

*"The Pentagon should withdraw recognition
of Wicca for readiness reasons."*

The American Military Should Stop Sanctioning the Wicca Religion

Robert L. Maginnis

Wicca is a modern term for a nature-worshipping religion. Some U.S. military bases have sanctioned the practice of Wicca among military recruits, just as they have historically employed chaplains and provided worship opportunities for Christians and members of other religious faiths. However, in June 1999 Georgia Congressman Bob Barr sought federal legislation banning the practice of Wicca on military bases. In the following viewpoint, Robert L. Maginnis argues that permitting the practice of the Wiccan religion damages military readiness, sets a precedent for any "fringe religion" to receive special military benefits, and is a direct affront to the majority of military personnel who are Christian or Jewish. Maginnis, a retired army lieutenant colonel, is a policy analyst for the Family Research Council, a conservative Christian research and educational organization.

As you read, consider the following questions:
1. What two general types of objections does Maginnis raise against the U.S. military's recognition of Wicca?
2. What are the main elements of Wiccan beliefs, according to the author?
3. How will military readiness be affected by official recognition of Wicca as a religion, according to Maginnis?

Excerpted from "Brewing Up Trouble: Wicca and the U.S. Military," by Robert L. Maginnis, Family Research Council, June 1999. Reprinted with permission.

Wicca received official recognition as a religion in 1996 from the Department of Defense (DOD). Today, there are at least five officially recognized military Wiccan congregations. The Pentagon should withdraw recognition of Wicca for readiness reasons.

Objections to the military's recognition of Wiccans fall in two categories: One, any fringe religion will now have to be granted special benefits by DOD; two, Wicca will undermine readiness factors such as military values, adherence to norms, willingness to kill, and recruitment and retention among the majority who hold a generally theistic worldview and regard witchcraft as an abomination.

The presence of minority religious views is not at issue in this controversy. Christians have served in the military in good faith with Muslims and Jews. These religions share a monotheistic and creationist consensus about the "law of nature and nature's God," as understood by the signers of the Declaration of Independence. Because Wicca represents a direct challenge to this widely shared theism, it would work against military discipline, order, and readiness.

Wicca represents a direct affront to Christian and Jewish teaching. The Bible condemns all forms of witchcraft and sorcery throughout the Old and New Testaments. . . .

U.S. Representative Bob Barr, a Georgia Republican, has asked the services to stop sanctioning the practice of witchcraft on military bases. Barr argues that allowing such celebrations sets "a dangerous precedent" that could lead to "all sorts of bizarre practices being supported by the military under the rubric of religion." Already, DOD has granted special benefits to other unconventional religious groups. Military members of the Native American church, for example, can legally use the illegal hallucinogenic drug peyote in their on-base religious ceremonies.

Military Support of Religion and Wicca

The U.S. military has always supported religion. [Marcia Jackson writes that] On July 29, 1775, George Washington "established the [chaplain] corps behind the idea that chaplains brought with them morality and ethics, and that was important in dealing with the forces." Today, the chaplain corps seeks to meet the needs of a very diverse uniformed population.

In 1998, the Defense Manpower Data Center found that most servicemembers identify with the Christian faith: 330,703 Roman Catholic; 252,855 Baptist (not including Southern Baptist); 43,056 Lutheran; 40,053 Methodist; 25,833 Southern Baptist Convention; 62,063 Protestant but with no denominational preference; and 96,259 labeling themselves Christians with no denominational preference. Twenty percent (283,836) have "no religious preference." Other religious preferences include Judaism (3,913), Muslim (4,080) and Buddhism (2,228). No Wiccans were identified.

Military regulations provide a process for religious groups without chaplains to gain access to base facilities for the purpose of conducting services. The qualification process requires that the group must be a recognized religion, military members must request the service and there must be evidence that assigned chaplains cannot meet the "specific theological/denominational requirements of [the] group." The U.S. government has recognized Wicca and has given it tax-exempt status as a religious organization. . . .

In August 1997, Wicca "high priest" David Oringderff, with the Sacred Well Congregation of San Antonio, helped set up the military's first Wicca Open Circle at Fort Hood near Austin, Texas. The Wicca Open Circle at Fort Hood has perhaps 300 members, about 100 of whom attend regularly. Oringderff has helped set up congregations at four other bases as well.

The Army defends its decision to support Wicca. *U.S. News and World Report* explains,

> For today's heterogeneous U.S. Army, the practice is basically business as usual. 'As far as we are concerned, they are a religious organization providing for the spiritual needs of our soldiers,' says Lt. Col. Benjamin Santos, Fort Hood spokesman, explaining the Army's decision to sanction the practice on bases.

Navy Captain Russell Gunter, executive director of the Armed Forces Chaplains Board at the Pentagon, also supports Wiccans at Fort Hood. The military is obligated, said Gunter, to respect the religious needs of its members without passing judgment.

Background of Wicca

Witchcraft, also known as Wicca, the craft, or the craft of the wise, is a religion with roots in the ancient pagan religions of northern Europe. Modern witchcraft is a reconstruction of the older versions, based on writings by anthropologist Margaret Murray (1863–1963)—*The Witch-Cult in Western Europe* (1921) and *The God of the Witches* (1933)—and by British civil servant and world traveler Gerald Gardner (1884–1964)—*Witchcraft Today* (1954) and *The Meaning of Witchcraft* (1959).

Llewellyn's 1999 Magickal Almanac explains,

> Wicca, as you practice the religion today, is a new religion, barely fifty years old. The techniques you use at present are not entirely what your elders practiced even thirty years ago. Of course, threads of 'what was' weave through the tapestry of 'what is now.' . . . [I]n no way can we replicate to perfection the precise circumstances of environment, society, culture, religion and magick a hundred years ago, or a thousand. Why would we want to? The idea is to go forward with the knowledge of the past, tempered by the tools of our own age.

"Contemporary witchcraft is so diverse and eclectic . . . that it is extremely difficult to accurately identify and define. In fact, it is almost impossible to state that all witches believe 'this or that,'" writes Craig Hawkins in the *Christian Research Journal*.

Wiccan Beliefs

Radical Feminism. Danya Ruttenburg wrote in the April 1998 *Sojourner* (a feminist magazine),

> [M]any feminists have certainly been attracted to paganism—the theological framework behind energy-channeling called magic or witchcraft. Women who practice paganism often describe it as a potent means of aligning their spiritual practice with their political beliefs.

> Though the modern practice has deep roots in a number of ancient traditions, the neo-pagan movement was initiated in England in the 1950s. It took hold in America in two separate, parallel movements—both as part of the non-Western spirituality explosion of the late 1960s, and with the concurrent development of goddess consciousness, in radical separatist feminism.

Russ Wise, with the Dallas-based Probe Ministries, adds,

In the world of witchcraft the goddess is the giver of life. Witchcraft holds a pantheistic view of God. God is nature. Therefore, God is in all things and all things are a part of God. However, this God is in actuality a goddess and predates the male God. The goddess is the giver of all life and is found in all of creation. This reshaping is nothing less than viewing man and his understanding of reality from a female-centered perspective which focuses on the Divine as being female. . . . The rise of the goddess is a direct assault on the patriarchal foundation of Christianity. This new feminist spirituality affirms bisexuality, lesbianism, homosexuality, and androgyny (through the expression of transvestitism).

"The Goddess religion is a conscious attempt to reshape culture," says Starhawk, a witch who works with a Catholic priest at the Institute of Creation Spirituality.

Where Will It End?

Recently, the chaplain's office at Fort Hood has led the way in using taxpayer dollars to provide information on the practice of witchcraft to interested soldiers. The rest of the military is following suit, and other chaplains' offices are now being used to support soldiers who want to be witches.

Even more alarmingly, the military is now drafting regulations allowing soldiers to use the powerful hallucinogenic drug peyote as part of a "religious" ritual. This decision could affect lives even more directly. What happens if a pilot hallucinates while flying, or if an artillery officer experiences a flashback while calculating coordinates?

This trend has very troubling implications if it is applied to other areas. For example, will armored divisions be forced to travel with sacrificial animals for Satanic rituals? Will Rastifarians demand the inclusion of ritualistic marijuana cigarettes in their rations?

Statement by U.S. Rep. Bob Barr, May 21, 1999.

Pacifist Tendencies. A June 1999 edition of the *Washington Post* identifies Wiccans as pacifists. Despite the "many varieties of Wicca," Wiccans in general accept a basic rule: "An ye harm none, do what ye will."

The Armed Forces Chaplains Board explains that many Wiccans "regard all living things as sacred" and consequently hold that the destruction of human and animal life is wrong. Others believe that "as Nature's way includes self-defense, they should participate in wars that they conscientiously consider to be just." Nonviolence, however, is the first principle of Wicca, according to a Wicca website:

> The harm which is to be regarded as unethical is gratuitous harm; *war, in general, is gratuitous harm* [emphasis added], although it is ethical to defend oneself and one's liberty when threatened by real and present danger, such as defense against invasion. . . .

Ethical Relativism. The Covenant of the Goddess, one of the largest and oldest Wiccan religious organizations in North America, states that evil is subjective: "[W]hat is good for one may be evil for another and vice versa."

Other examples of this relativistic view abound. Additional Wiccan websites, for instance, make the following claims:

- "Wiccans rely on their own judgement [sic] to create their own morals, and ideals. . . . We interact with our gods on a regular basis, and we take their power into ourselves during our rituals. We know and feel our Gods, so we don't believe, we know."
- "Witches consider no act immoral unless it is harmful."
- "Witches have no specific taboos against speaking any particular words, consensual sexual acts among individuals capable of rational consent, or breaking laws they know to be unjust.". . .

Implications for Military Readiness

- Cohesive units are made of soldiers who subscribe to similar values. For the military, there are clear rights and wrongs, not maybes. Wiccans, on the other hand, are noted for their ethical relativism.
- Wiccans subscribe to a radical feminist worldview that supports sexually deviant behavior such as bisexuality and homosexuality, both of which are illegal in the military.
- A "Wiccan warrior" is an oxymoron. Wiccans tend to be pacifists, which may be all right for medics but not for infantrymen.
- The military has already allowed peyote smoking to accommodate Native Americans, and there are a growing number of cases of Muslim soldiers appealing decisions about headgear, dietary requirements and special holi-

days. Exceptions for every group will drain limited resources and distract from the military's primary mission of preparing to fight. The military should embrace corporate rather than individual interests.

• Today's military is overwhelmingly Christian. The Bible labels witchcraft as an abomination. Accommodating witches who engage in behaviors that are antithetical to the "law of nature and nature's God" will cause unit friction, undermine morale, and impair recruitment and retention.

Unfortunately, the modern military has embraced tolerance for virtually every bizarre practice. It's past time for Congress to exercise its constitutional obligation to stop the Pentagon's willingness to sacrifice national defense in order to accommodate political correctness. The armed forces should focus on readiness.

"Does it hurt anyone to allow Witches to practice their religion in the military? From . . . personal experience, I can definitely say no."

The American Military Should Not Ban the Wicca Religion

Chad Anctil

Chad Anctil is a veteran of the U.S. Navy who served for six years before being honorably discharged. He is also a practitioner of Wicca, a nature-worshipping religion that traces its roots to ancient times, and whose members are known as witches. In the following viewpoint, he argues that his religion was never secret from his military peers and superiors, and that it never affected his performance or his unit's morale or combat readiness. Those who wish to ban the practice of the Wiccan religion on American military bases are motivated by religious prejudice and do not fully understand the American tradition of religious freedom, he concludes.

As you read, consider the following questions:

1. How did people in the military who worked directly with the author react to his religion?
2. What should be the main issue concerning witches in the military, according to Anctil?
3. Did Anctil receive any special treatment because of his religion, in his view?

Reprinted, with permission, from "A Veteran Witch Speaks Out," by Chad Anctil, July 27, 1999, as found at the following URL: www.celticcrow.com/perspectives/essat72799.html (as downloaded 10/2/00).

My name is Chad Anctil. I am a 6-year US Navy veteran. I served during the Gulf War, and during my enlistment I received many awards and decorations, including two Admirals' Letters and a Commendation from the Commander of the Pacific Fleet. I served proudly and I was considered an excellent sailor by my command, receiving an Honorable Discharge at the end of my enlistment. I was also a practicing Witch.

Everyone in my command knew I was a Witch—I never hid it from anyone. During my six years, only three people ever had a problem with my religion. Everyone knew me, and I made sure they knew what Witchcraft was, and what it wasn't. No one thought I was a Devil worshipper, no one was afraid to be my roommate in the barracks, and I had lots of friends and no real enemies. It's true, there was no place for me to 'officially' worship on base, and there was no local circle or group I could connect with, but I was allowed my candles and my moonlit rituals undisturbed—people knew about it, and no one cared.

Witches at Fort Hood

Naturally I was very interested when, a few months ago [in 1999], an article appeared in a Texas newspaper, talking about a group of Witches who were allowed to openly practice their religion on a US Army installation—Ft. Hood, in Texas. In truth, this was not big news—the Witches of Ft. Hood Open Circle had been given permission to practice, as well as a chaplain, over two years before the article ran, and save for a few unhappy local Christians, there had not been any problems at all. The article was positive in nature, and I don't believe it was written to stir up controversy—it was just a newspaper article.

Enter Rep. Bob Barr of Georgia and the 'Religious Right', and their battle to stop Satan in his tracks by stopping the 'evil' practice of Witchcraft on military bases worldwide. The reasons given were varied—Witches believe in harming none, so they don't belong in uniform (I believe 'Thou Shalt Not Kill' is written somewhere in the bible—it must be towards the back); the objection to spending 'taxpayer money' to allow Witches to practice their faith (I don't fully understand this one, since the Witches don't have a full time chaplain—they borrow one when they need him—and they aren't even asking for a church or chapel like all the other religions have—they worship in an open field, and like it that way). Also, my personal favorite: If the army let Witches practice their religion, they would have to carry sacrificial animals into combat for Satanists and marijuana for Rastafarians. I won't even comment on the ridiculousness of this one.

Slow Acceptance of Pagans

"Many people have misconceptions of modern Paganism and, unfortunately, mistake it for Satanism or other dark and threatening religion," said Navy Petty Officer 3rd Class James Schofield, stationed in Sasebo, Japan. "People see a pentacle and think, 'Oh, the devil.'". . .

Paganism is defined by the U.S. Army Chaplain's Handbook as a reconstruction of nature worship, much like ancient tribal worship of Europe. Pagans believe in an ultimate divine presence in the universe which contains both male and female forms, the goddess and the god, and is present in the natural world and inside each person. . . .

But despite growing tolerance, most military Pagans still are reluctant to reveal their religious faith to others. Acceptance of Paganism, they said, is a slow process.

Jennifer Correro, *Air Force Times*, November 1997.

Never mind that every other religion is allowed to practice, from Christian to Buddhist to Hindu, and never mind the argument of Religious Freedom—according to Mr. Barr, that doesn't exist for members of the US Armed Forces, even though they are ready to lay down their lives to defend it.

After the initial coverage of the issue, I thought that this would be a minor political diversion, a few days of media coverage, and it would die. After all, the military has no intention to change the policy—Wicca and Witchcraft have been in the Chaplains' Handbook since the late 1980's, and the whole thing seemed so ridiculous; to be arguing about Religious Freedom in America, and using 16th century logic to do it! How wrong I was.

After almost 2 full months of controversy, the battle still

rages. Several Christian organizations are calling for a boycott of the army(!!) and articles and editorials still dot the news—some exceedingly positive, while others seem to take their information—and prejudices—straight from the Salem Witch Trials. Now, with a renewed media interest in Witchcraft due to the film 'The Blair Witch Project', the issue seems to be coming to the surface again. . . .

The Main Issue

To me, the main issue here should be this: Does it hurt anyone to allow Witches to practice their religion in the military? From six years of personal experience, I can definitely say no. It did nothing to combat readiness, it did nothing to morale. There just wasn't an issue, and no one made it an issue. Once, a crew member who was born-again Christian went to the command, saying he was offended by my books on Witchcraft. The command told him if I got rid of my books, his bible had to go, too—he saw their point of view on religious freedom and that was the end of the problem. I did my job just like everyone else, and I did it well. Only once in 6 years did I receive 'special treatment' due to my religion—I was given Samhain (Halloween) off—but I also volunteered to stand Christmas duty to allow someone who celebrated Christmas to be home with their family. I am sure that the Witches at Ft. Hood—and all over the military—are the same way, just regular soldiers and sailors who do their jobs, have friends and families, and worship the God and Goddess. There really should be no issue, and we should all work together towards a day when there is none.

Periodical Bibliography

The following articles have been selected to supplement the diverse views presented in this chapter. Addresses are provided for periodicals not indexed in the *Readers' Guide to Periodical Literature*, the *Alternative Press Index*, the *Social Sciences Index*, or the *Index to Legal Periodicals and Books*.

Barbara Beckwith — "Reviving the Religious Freedom Restoration Act," *St. Anthony Messenger*, February 1998. Available from 1615 Republic St., Cincinnati, OH 45210.

Joan Brown Campbell et al. — "Religious Liberty Requires Unceasing Vigilance," *USA Today*, September 1996.

Stephen L. Carter — "The Freedom to Resist," *Christianity Today*, June 12, 2000.

Christian Century — "New Legislation on Religious Freedom," August 2–9, 2000.

E.J. Dionne Jr. — "Bridging the Church-State Divide," *Washington Post National Weekly Edition*, October 11, 1999. Available from UMI, 300 N. Zeeb Rd., Ann Arbor, MI 48106.

Steve France — "Establishment Pause: Religious Freedom Meets Anti-Discrimination Law," *Reason*, July 1999.

S.C. Gwynne-Killeen — "I Saluted a Witch," *Time*, July 5, 1999.

John Ratliff — "Witch Hunt," *Texas Monthly*, October 1999.

Christopher Reed — "Pay Things of the Gods," *World Press Review*, June 2000.

Jeffrey Rosen — "Is Nothing Secular?" *New York Times Magazine*, January 30, 2000.

Carl E. Schneider — "Justification by Faith," *Hastings Center Report*, January/February 1999.

David O. Stewart — "Power Surge," *ABA Journal*, September 1997. Available from 750 N. Lakeshore Dr., Chicago, IL 60611.

David Van Biema — "Faith or Healing?" *Time*, August 31, 1998.

M. Victor Westberg — "When Faith Heals," *Liberty*, May/June 1998. Available from the North American Division of the Seventh-Day Adventist Church, 12501 Old Columbia Pike, Silver Spring, MD 20904-6600 or online at www.libertymagazine.org.

Chapter Preface

Public schools are the tool with which American society transmits its knowledge and values to the next generation. They are also the place where students of many different religious beliefs gather together. Because of this commingling of faiths, schools have long been the setting for the debate over the place of religion in American society and its institutions. One flashpoint of this debate is school prayer.

In the first half of the twentieth century many American public schools often began the school day with a recited prayer. One such prayer, composed by the New York State Board of Regents so as to be nondenominational, read as follows: "Almighty God, we acknowledge our dependence upon Thee, and we beg Thy blessings upon us, our parents, our teachers, and our country." In 1962, however, the Supreme Court ruled in the case of *Engel v. Vitale* that such state-sponsored prayers in public schools were unconstitutional because they violated the First Amendment, which reads in part: "Congress shall make no law respecting an establishment of religion, or prohibiting the free exercise thereof." Many people then and since have deplored the ruling, arguing that religion was being driven from public schools. Supporters of the 1962 ruling argued that students could still pray, but that schools could not create a coercive environment by endorsing or sanctioning a particular set of words or prayers. The issue of school prayer has returned to the Supreme Court periodically since then, including a 2000 case in which the Supreme Court forbade students from sponsoring and leading prayers before high school football games.

The school prayer question is just one of several issues concerning the status of religion in the nation's public schools. President Bill Clinton declared in 1995 that the First Amendment "does not convert our schools into religion-free zones." However, teachers and administrators are continually attempting to maintain a balance between avoiding "establishment of religion" and permitting religion's "free exercise." The viewpoints in this chapter examine school prayer and other issues.

"By ignoring religion, [schools] . . . are hostile to religion and discriminate against it."

Public Schools Should Include More Religion in the Curriculum

Warren A. Nord

Warren A. Nord teaches philosophy and religion at the University of North Carolina at Chapel Hill and is the author of *Religion and American Education: Rethinking a National Dilemma*. In the following viewpoint, he discusses his findings from reviewing high school textbooks and national content standards being developed by teachers and others. He argues that religion is being systematically excluded from public school curricula. Such exclusion impoverishes the education students receive and betrays a hostility to religion. The lack of religious content in public education should be a concern to all people concerned about America's schools regardless of how conservative or liberal they are in religion or politics, he concludes.

As you read, consider the following questions:
1. What three main subject areas does Nord focus on in his discussion of religion in the curriculum?
2. What observations does the author make about his own students concerning their religious knowledge?
3. What secular reasons for supporting the teaching of religion in public schools does Nord list?

Excerpted from "Religion-Free Texts: Getting an Illiberal Education," by Warren A. Nord. Reprinted with permission from the July 14–21, 1999, issue of the *Christian Century*. Copyright 1999 Christian Century Foundation.

In the current culture wars, religious liberals tend to ally themselves with the educational establishment against those on the Religious Right who are attacking the public schools. In politics and theology, I line up with the left. Nonetheless, I believe with the right that public education is hostile to religion—not least to liberal religion. The problem isn't the absence of school prayers. Schools respect the religious liberty of students in prohibiting religious exercises. There is no hostility to religion in that. The problem is that systematically excluding religious voices from the curriculum makes public education fundamentally illiberal—something that, ironically, most liberals fail to see.

During the past few years I've reviewed 82 high school textbooks in a variety of subjects—history, economics, home economics, literature, health and the sciences—for their treatment of religion. I've also read the national content standards that have been developed for K–12 education over the past decade [the 1990s] by thousands of scholars, teachers and representatives of professional organizations. To keep my discussion manageable I will comment only on high school texts and standards in three subject areas: economics, the sciences and history. But the problems we find here cut across the curriculum at all levels of education.

• Economics. The scriptures of all religious traditions address justice and the moral dimensions of social and economic life, as does much recent moral theology—from the social gospel through liberation theology. Most mainline Christian denominations and many ecumenical agencies have official statements on economics and justice. Central to scripture and this literature is the claim that to understand the economic domain of life we must apply moral and religious categories to it. Yet in the 4,400 pages of the ten economics texts I reviewed, all of the references to religion add up to only two pages, and all are to distant history. In the 47 pages of the national economics standards there are no references at all to religious ways of understanding economics.

Neither the texts nor the standards address poverty as a moral or spiritual problem; indeed, they say little about poverty at all. They are silent about the relationship between the First World and the Third. They ignore the effect of economics and technology on the environment. They are oblivious to the moral problems of a consumer culture. They ask no questions about dehumanizing work. They emphasize the importance of the profit motive and competition, and never mention that profits may be excessive or that competition may have its costs. They never speak of the dignity of people, the sacredness of nature or our obligations to any larger community (or to God).

The problem isn't just what's left out, however; it's also what's included. The texts and national standards teach neoclassical economic theory. According to this theory, economics is a "value-free" science, and the economic world can be defined in terms of the competition for scarce resources between self-interested individuals with unlimited wants. Values are subjective preferences. Decisions should be made according to cost-benefit analyses that maximize whatever it is we value and that leave no room in the equation for duties, the sacred or the unquantifiable dimensions of life. Economics and religion seem to be entirely separate realms.

My findings confirm what sociologist Robert Wuthnow discovered in his study of American religious life: people divorce economics from religion. When "asked if their religious beliefs had influenced their choice of a career, most of the people I have interviewed in recent years—Christians and non-Christians alike—said no. Asked if they thought of their work as a calling, most said no. Asked if they understood the concept of stewardship, most said no. Asked how religion did influence their work lives or thoughts about money, most said the two were completely separate."

The way we teach economics contributes to the growing secularization and demoralization of economic life. Indeed, it is virtually impossible to reconcile the understanding of human nature, values and economics found in the texts and the national standards with that of any religious tradition. . . .

Positions on Evolution

• Science. The attention given to the conflict over biological evolution distorts the issue by making it seem as if there are just two sides—the evolutionists and the fundamentalist creationists. Actually, there are a variety of religious positions, liberal as well as conservative. Yes, religious liberals have accepted evolution pretty much from the time Charles Darwin first proposed it, but in contrast to Darwin many of them believe that evolution is purposeful and that nature has a spiritual dimension. Darwin stated in his *Autobiography* that there is no more design to be found in nature than in the course which the wind blows, and the National Association of Biology Teachers and the National Science Association have decided to align themselves with his view that evolution is purposeless. This is what students learn in biology classes—though the religious implications of evolution are rarely addressed explicitly. Biology texts and the national science standards both ignore not only fundamentalist creationism but also those more liberal religious ways of interpreting evolution found in process theology, creation spirituality, intelligent-design theory and much feminist and postmodern theology.

There is also a good deal of speculation now among scientists, theologians and philosophers about cosmic evolution, for there appears to be impressive evidence that the universe was fine-tuned to produce life. Life is extraordinarily complicated and improbable, and if conditions had been different in only the very smallest degree the universe would have been lifeless. It is possible to argue that the development of life was, in some way, programmed from the beginning. A creator God seems the most reasonable explanation for this—or so it is often argued. In fact, the whole Big Bang theory has often been taken to be of some theological significance. Yet physics texts and the science standards are silent on all of this. . . .

Many liberal theologians have held that science and religion are conceptual apples and oranges, as it were. According to this "two worlds" view, they should have nothing to do with each other. One is about mechanics, the other about meaning. In recent decades, however, there has been a growing movement among theologians (and among some scientists) to see relations between science and religion. Theologians quite properly use scientific insights to shape their convictions about nature, and scientists—at least those working at the level of basic theory—are inevitably drawn to theological considerations. But because the national science standards and the textbooks have nothing to say about the relationship between science and religion, students will assume that science is competent to provide a complete picture of nature—a claim deeply controversial for religious liberals as well as conservatives.

Religion Disappears from History

• History. It is widely thought that students learn about religion when they study history. Indeed, the textbooks and the national history standards say a good deal about religion—yet they don't take religion as seriously as they should. World history texts typically devote about three pages to explaining the origins, basic teachings and early development of each of the great world religions. But religion virtually disappears from the texts as we page past the 18th century or, in American histories, the Civil War. The world histories devote about 1 percent of their pages to religion after 1750. Each of the American histories I reviewed gave more space to the Watergate scandal than to all post–Civil War religion. . . .

Perhaps most important, while the great Western religions have held that God is revealed in the events and shape of history, none of the texts discuss religious interpretations of history. The texts clearly (and uncritically) assume that history is a secular discipline and that secular explanations are adequate.

Avoiding All Discussion of Religion

Health and sex education and home economics texts and curricula avoid any discussion of religious ways of thinking about sexuality, marriage, abortion and homosexuality. While some literature anthologies are organized chronologically and so include some religious literature, most include only recent secular literature. Civics textbooks discuss government, law, rights and justice without any substantive discussion of religion. The growing character education movement in public education bends over backwards to avoid any reference to religion's role in nurturing virtues and values.

By ignoring religion, the texts and standards are hostile to religion and discriminate against it. There are a variety of ways of making sense of the world. Many of us accept one or another religious interpretation of reality; others accept one or another secular interpretation. The differences between us often cut deep. Yet public schools systematically teach students to think about the world in secular ways only. They don't even bother to note that there are religious alternatives.

Embracing Religion's Moral Power

Religion already is a part of the curriculum. It is interwoven into motivations for exploration and wars as well as peace; it is a theme that runs through much of our literary and musical heritage; and it is a predominant topic in philosophy. Rather than fearing religion's presence, we should reach out and embrace its power.

I recently had an opportunity to visit a school with a room set aside where volunteers could interact with and counsel students who had been assigned an in-school suspension for some behavioral infraction. The volunteers had decorated the room with sayings from Gandhi, Jesus, Mohammed, Buddha, Martin Luther King, Jr., Moses, and others who have contributed to the moral conversation of our world societies. The presence of so many diverse voices all speaking about the value of truth, honesty, respect, and responsibility created a powerful montage and at the same time represented the essence of what religion in the schools can and should be.

Barbara McEwan, *USA Today*, May 1997.

Some argue that a secular curriculum is religiously neutral so long as it doesn't overtly attack religion. But this view is naive. For some time now, people have rightly argued that ignoring black history and women's literature (as texts and curricula have traditionally done) has been anything but neutral. Rather, it betrays a prejudice; it is discriminatory. And so it is with religion. Indeed, it is more dishonest and dangerous to ignore religion than it is to attack it overtly. An overt attack at least makes students aware of potential tensions and conflicts between religious and secular ways of thinking and living. It makes them realize that what they are taught is sometimes controversial.

No doubt much of what students learn in their secular studies is compatible with religion. The problem lies less with the "facts" they are taught than with the philosophical assumptions, the governing worldview, with which they are taught to interpret the various subjects. They learn particular—always secular—ways of thinking about the content. The assumption is that secular perspectives are adequate to getting at the truth about any subject. The cumulative effect of this approach is that public education nurtures a secular mentality. Religion is intellectually compartmentalized and, therefore, marginalized—though this is almost always done implicitly (and often, no doubt, unintentionally).

It is true that most students continue to believe in God. But God has little to do with how they think about the world or how they live their lives. The vast majority of my students at the University of North Carolina at Chapel Hill are religiously illiterate. Perhaps worst of all, they are convinced that religion is a matter of irrational faith, and that when we talk about evidence, arguments and reason we must be talking about science.

Why don't liberals see a problem in this? Some continue to believe, mistakenly, that our constitutional "wall of separation" between church and state prohibits serious study of religion in public schools. No doubt many are concerned that in a religiously pluralistic society it is too difficult—and too controversial—to put religion on the educational agenda. And, of course, there is no vision of what an adequate treatment of religion might look like.

Perhaps more important, our cultural wars have led to tactical alliances between religious and secular liberals, who wish to present a united front against those who would make America into a Christian country and our schools into Christian schools. As James Davison Hunter has persuasively argued, the most important battle lines seem to separate liberals from conservatives, not religious folk from secular folk.

Liberal Reasons for Teaching Religion

There are good liberal, secular reasons for incorporating the serious study of religion into the curriculum of public schools. First, a good liberal education should expose students to the major ways that humankind has devised for thinking about what is most important. Some of those ways are religious. Religions continue to possess a great deal of intellectual vitality, even in our secular culture. They continue to ask and provide answers to those existential questions on which any educated person must reflect. Theologians—conservative and liberal—continue to provide alternatives to secular ways of thinking about the world.

Second, there are liberal political reasons for taking religion seriously. When we are deeply divided about some matter of importance, public schools must not educationally disenfranchise a significant segment of the public by ignoring its ideas and ideals. Because we are deeply divided about politics, public schools should not side with Democrats or Republicans but should give students some sense of what it has meant, and continues to mean, to be either. We are also deeply divided about religion. Justice requires that religious citizens not be educationally disenfranchised.

We now widely acknowledge the importance of giving oppressed subcultures a voice in the curriculum and think that their history and literature should be taken seriously. Hardly any groups are now so ignored in the curriculum as are religious subcultures—which provide many Americans with their deepest sense of identity and meaning.

Third, there are liberal constitutional arguments for requiring, not just permitting, the study of religion in public schools. Ever since 1947, when the Supreme Court first applied the First Amendment's establishment clause to the states in *Everson v. Board of Education*, the court has held that government must be neutral on matters of religion. This commitment to neutrality has become the liberal position on church and state. (Conservatives have generally held that it is permissible for the state to promote at least nonsectarian religion.)

Of course, neutrality is a two-edged sword—as the court has also made clear. If the state can't promote religion, neither can it denigrate it: As Justice Hugo Black put it in *Everson*, "State power is no more to be used so as to handicap religions than it is to favor them." Writing for the court in *Abington v. Schempp* (1963), Justice Tom Clark held that public schools cannot establish a "religion of secularism," preferring "those who believe in no religion over those who do believe." In a concurring opinion, Justice Arthur Goldberg warned that an "untutored devotion to the concept of neutrality" can lead to a "pervasive devotion to the secular and a passive, or even active, hostility to the religious."

This is just what has happened. An "untutored" conception of neutrality has led educators to conflate secular education with religiously neutral education. The only way to be truly neutral when all ground is contested is to be fair to the alternatives.

How to incorporate the serious study of religion into the curriculum is, of course, controversial and complex. But religious voices (conservative and liberal, Christian and non-Christian) must be included in the curricular conversation, not to save religion, but to be consistent with our educational, political and constitutional principles.

*"The probability that attempts to teach
about religion will go horribly wrong
should caution public schools to make haste
very slowly in this area."*

Public Schools Should Not Include More Religion in the Curriculum

Edd Doerr

Edd Doerr is president of the American Humanist Association. In the following viewpoint, he argues that despite
progress made by schools in protecting students from having
religious activities imposed upon them, problems remain,
such as inappropriate use of religious material in music
classes. He argues that public schools are not hostile to religion, and that the lack of religious content in public school
curricula is due to low demand, lack of time, and the political
complexities and problems inherent in teaching religion in a
truly neutral fashion. Doerr concludes that schools face more
pressing problems in reforming their curricula, including the
teaching of science, foreign languages, and other subjects
that should receive a higher priority than teaching religion.

As you read, consider the following questions:
1. What is prohibited and required by guidelines issued by
   the Department of Education, according to Doerr?
2. What questions need to be answered before religion can
   be fairly taught in school, according to the author?
3. What special function do public schools serve, according
   to Doerr?

Excerpted from "Religion and Public Education," by Edd Doerr, *Phi Delta
Kappan*, November 1998. Reprinted with permission.

The U.S. Commission on Civil Rights held the first of three projected hearings on "Schools and Religion." Most of the 16 experts who spoke at the hearing (including this writer, I must disclose) agreed that the relevant Supreme Court rulings and other developments have pretty much brought public education into line with the religious neutrality required by the First Amendment and the increasingly pluralistic nature of our society. A fair balance has been established between the free exercise rights of students and the constitutional obligation of neutrality.

The speakers attributed the current reasonably satisfactory situation to 50 years of appropriate Supreme Court rulings plus two specific developments: passage by Congress in 1984 of the Equal Access Law, which allows student-initiated religious groups or other groups not related to the curriculum to meet, without school sponsorship, during noninstructional time; and the U.S. Department of Education's issuance in August 1995 of guidelines on "Religious Expression in Public Schools.". . .

The guidelines grew out of a document titled "Religion in the Public Schools: A Joint Statement of Current Law," issued in April 1995 by a broad coalition of 36 religious and civil liberties groups. The statement declared that the Constitution "permits much private religious activity in and around the public schools and does not turn the schools into religion-free zones." The statement went on to detail what is and is not permissible in the schools. . . .

School Guidelines

The guidelines, based on 50 years of court rulings . . . on common sense, and on a healthy respect for American religious diversity, have proved useful to school boards, administrators, teachers, students, parents, and religious leaders. Following is a brief summary.

Permitted—"Purely private religious speech by students"; nondisruptive individual or group prayer, grace before meals, religious literature reading; student speech about religion or anything else, including that intended to persuade, so long as it stops short of harassment; private baccalaureate services; teaching about religion; inclusion by students of religious matter in written or oral assignments where not inappropriate; student distribution of religious literature on the same terms as other material not related to school curricula or activities; some degree of right to excusal from lessons objectionable on religious or conscientious grounds, subject to applicable state laws; off-campus released time or dismissed time for religious instruction; teaching civic values; student-initiated "Equal Access" religious groups of secondary students during noninstructional time.

Prohibited—School endorsement of any religious activity or doctrine; coerced participation in religious activity; engaging in or leading student religious activity by teachers, coaches, or officials acting as advisors to student groups; allowing harassment of or religious imposition on "captive audiences"; observing holidays as religious events or promoting such observance; imposing restrictions on religious expression more stringent than those on nonreligious expression; allowing religious instruction by outsiders on school premises during the school day.

Required—"Official neutrality regarding religious activity.". . .

Problem Areas

As good and useful as the guidelines are, there remain three areas in which problems continue: proselytizing by adults in public schools, music programs that fall short of the desired neutrality, and teaching appropriately about religion.

There are conservative evangelists, such as Jerry Johnston and the Rev. Jerry Falwell, who have described public schools as "mission fields." In communities from coast to coast, proselytizers from well-financed national organizations, such as Campus Crusade and Young Life, and volunteer "youth pastors" from local congregations have operated in public schools for years. They use a variety of techniques: presenting assembly programs featuring "role model" athletes, getting permission from school officials to contact students one-on-one in cafeterias and hallways, volunteering as unpaid teaching aides, and using substance abuse lectures or assemblies to gain access to students. It is not uncommon for these activities to have the tacit approval of local school authorities. Needless to say, these operations tend to take place more often in smaller, more religiously homogeneous communities than in larger, more pluralistic ones.

Why Schools Should Be Religion-Free Zones

I advance a four-point argument to show why the public schools should be religion-free zones:

1. *Government compels school attendance.* Minor children not attending recognized private schools or undergoing home schooling must attend public schools. This obligation is enforced by truancy law. . . . It follows that the government must exercise extraordinary care in its stewardship of the children attending public schools, because their presence is in response to threats of government coercion.

2. *Public schools bring together students of every imaginable faith, and of none.*

3. *Constitutional issues aside, there are now too many creeds to support them all equally, as Christianity and Judaism were (improperly) supported in the past.* Even if we *wanted* to go back to the "good old days," in a polycreedal society there are just too many faiths. Shall we close the schools for Ramadan; for Diwali, the five-day Hindu festival of lights; on November 12, the birthday of Bahaullah, venerated by the Baha'is; and on April 13, the Sikh New Year? . . . No, in a polycreedal society the best government institutions can hope to provide *equally* to *every* creed is benign neglect.

4. *It is impossible to reconcile the contradictory doctrines that may be held literally—and often defended with dogmatic intensity—by adherents of different faiths.* There can be a broad spectrum of subjects on which children who belong to one or another religious group hold unorthodox—and constitutionally protected—views. In such situations government is helpless to do anything but retreat from the contended topic area. This insight has profound implications for issues such as evolution and teaching about religion. Simply put, religion is too hot for public schools to handle.

Thomas W. Flynn, *Free Inquiry*, Spring 1996.

Religious music in the public school curriculum, in student concerts and theatrical productions, and at graduation ceremonies has long been a thorny issue. As Secretary of Education Richard Riley's 1995 and 1998 guidelines and court rulings have made clear, schools may offer instruction about religion, but they must remain religiously neutral and may not formally celebrate religious special days. What then about religious music, which looms large in the history of music?

As a vocal and instrumental musician in high school and college and as an amateur adult musician in both secular and religious musical groups, I feel qualified to address this issue. There should be no objection to the inclusion of religious music in the academic study of music and in vocal and instrumental performances, as long as the pieces are selected primarily for their musical or historical value, as long as the program is not predominantly religious, and as long as the principal purpose and effect of the inclusion is secular. Thus there should be no objection to inclusion in a school production of religious music by Bach or Aaron Copland's arrangements of such 19th-century songs as "Simple Gifts" or "Let Us Gather by the River." What constitutes "musical or historical value" is, of course, a matter of judgment and controversy among musicians and scholars, so there can be no simple formula for resolving all conflicts.

Certain activities should clearly be prohibited. Public school choral or instrumental ensembles should not be used to provide music for church services or celebrations, though a school ensemble might perform a secular music program in a church or synagogue as part of that congregation's series of secular concerts open to the public and not held in conjunction with a worship service. Sectarian hymns should not be included in graduation ceremonies; a Utah case dealing with that subject has been turned down for Supreme Court review. Students enrolled in music programs for credit should not be compelled to participate in performances that are not primarily religiously neutral.

Teaching About Religion

As for teaching about religion, while one can agree with the Supreme Court that public schools may, and perhaps should, alleviate ignorance in this area in a fair, balanced, objective, neutral, academic way, getting from theory to practice is far from easy. The difficulties should be obvious. Teachers are very seldom adequately trained to teach about religion.

There are no really suitable textbooks on the market. Educators and experts on religion are nowhere near agreement on precisely what ought to be taught, how much should be taught and at what grade levels, and whether such material should be integrated into social studies classes, when appropriate, or offered in separate courses, possibly electives. And those who complain most about the relative absence of religion from the curriculum seem to be less interested in neutral academic study than in narrower sectarian teaching.

Textbooks and schools tend to slight religion not out of hostility toward religion but because of low demand, lack of time (if you add something to the curriculum, what do you take out to make room for it?), lack of suitable materials, and fear of giving offense or generating unpleasant controversy.

The following questions hint at the complexity of the subject. Should teaching about religion deal only with the bright side of it and not with the dark side (religious wars, controversies, bigotry, persecutions, and so on)? Should instruction deal only with religions within the U.S., or should it include religions throughout the world? Should it be critical or uncritical? Should all religious traditions be covered or only some? Should the teaching deal only with sacred books—and, if so, which ones and which translations? How should change and development in all religions be dealt with?

To be more specific, should we teach only about the Pilgrims and the first Thanksgiving, or also about the Salem witch trials and the execution of Quakers? Should schools mention only the Protestant settlers in British North America or also deal with French Catholic missionaries in Canada, Michigan, and Indiana and with the Spanish Catholics and secret Jews in our Southwest? Should we mention that Martin Luther King was a Baptist minister but ignore the large number of clergy who defended slavery and then segregation on Biblical grounds?

Should teaching about religion cover such topics as the evolution of Christianity and its divisions, the Crusades, the Inquisition, the religious wars after the Reformation, the long history of anti-Semitism and other forms of murderous bigotry, the role of religion in social and international tensions (as in Ireland, in the former Yugoslavia, and in India and Pakistan), the development in the U.S. of religious liberty and church/state separation, denominations and religions founded in the U.S., controversies over women's rights and reproductive rights, or newer religious movements?

The probability that attempts to teach about religion will go horribly wrong should caution public schools to make haste very slowly in this area. In my opinion, other curricular inadequacies—less controversial ones, such as those in the fields of science, social studies, foreign languages, and world literature—should be remedied before we tackle the thorniest subject of all.

And let us not forget that the American landscape has no shortage of houses of worship, which generally include religious education as one of their main functions. Nothing prevents these institutions from providing all the teaching about religion they might desire.

The late Supreme Court Justice William Brennan summed up the constitutional ideal rather neatly in his concurring opinion in *Abington Township S.D. v. Schempp*, the 1963 school prayer case: "It is implicit in the history and character of American public education that the public schools serve a uniquely public function: the training of American citizens in an atmosphere free of parochial, divisive, or separatist influence of any sort—an atmosphere in which children may assimilate a heritage common to all American groups and religions. This is a heritage neither theistic nor atheistic, but simply civic and patriotic."

"School prayer . . . created negative feelings for many students who took years to finally realize that they were not deficient because of their belief or nonbelief."

School Prayers Are Unfair to Students

Jeff Archer

In the early 1960s a series of Supreme Court rulings banned the practice of prayers and Bible readings in public school classrooms. Many have decried these rulings and have argued that reintroducing prayer in public schools would foster unity and morality among students. In the following viewpoint, Jeff Archer recalls that when he was in school, the practice of school prayer divided students on religious grounds and stigmatized Jews and other members of religious minorities. Archer is president of the Atheist Coalition of San Diego, California.

As you read, consider the following questions:
1. How does the author respond to the contention that reintroducing school prayer would reduce lawlessness?
2. What religious differences were revealed by school recitations of the Lord's Prayer, according to Archer?
3. What happened to Archer and his classmates when school prayer was discontinued?

Reprinted, with permission, from "A Case Against Prayer in the Classroom," by Jeff Archer, *The San Diego Union-Tribune*, June 1, 2000.

S ince 1963, school-led prayers have been unconstitutional in the United States. In the last few years, however, there have been those who have made a case for the reintroduction of prayer into public schools. Their reasons for this regression are as varied as their arguments.

I have read that pro-prayer advocates maintain that violence and lawlessness in our society will diminish considerably if students are allowed a moment of prayer prior to their school day. However, I have never read any data that were compiled to enable anyone to make such an assertion.

Remembering School Prayers

Instead of attempting to re-evaluate the arguments of both sides of the issue, I would like to take us back to those pre-1963 idyllic days when American students recited the Lord's Prayer at the beginning of the school day. Instead of prayer being a unified force which aided students in good citizenship, it was a dividing ritual to many.

Until I was 16 years old, I participated in the ritual of prayer at school, despite my having no religion. At the time, I did not realize that the prayer was only for Christians, and no one ever challenged the exclusivity of the religious background of the Lord's Prayer. I learned the words in first grade as the teacher led the prayer.

It was not long, however, until I realized something was amiss. In my area, most people were of the Roman Catholic faith. Their prayer differed from that of the Protestants, which added a line to the Catholic version. When the Catholics stopped, the few Protestants in the class would continue under the skeptical eyes of the Catholics who considered the Protestant version of the prayer to be blasphemous. I can remember Catholic kids on the school bus admonishing the Protestants for their version of the prayer. "What are you Protestants protesting?" asked one enlightened youngster. Actions such as these were commonplace, not just an aberration.

More apparent, however, was the curious look on the faces of the few Jewish students as they stood in silence while all the Christians, Catholic and Protestant alike, recited the words. They were taken to task by a unified front of Christians on the playground for their non-acquiesence. At least the Christian kids did not argue among themselves on this point.

Even worse was the look on the faces of some of the teachers. I can recall a few who were Roman Catholic who appeared to be disturbed when the Protestants recited their version. A situation in which a teacher was able to show his/her own religious prejudice was in force. Such actions are not conducive for an astute learning atmosphere for students.

During the time of legal school prayer, millions of black kids were not allowed to pray with millions of white kids. I heard little about this inequity from the teachers or those in the clergy who took school prayer as a God-given right of Americans.

One morning, during my sophomore year of high school, my homeroom teacher made an announcement that was devoid of emotion or explanation. He told the class, "As of today, there will be no more school prayer in the classroom." He then went on to give the students an assignment.

A Sense of Relief

There was a sense of relief among the students. Most, believers and nonbelievers alike, had considered the prayer a time of giving lip-service to something they did not feel was important in the classroom. Today, we forget those emotions and have re-written history to blame all our ills on the removing of prayer from the classroom.

School prayer was a divisive instrument which added to the creation of partitions among students in other areas such as race, ethnic background and social mores. Students, especially those younger ones, are very susceptible to criticism and not being a part of the mainstream. School prayer enhanced divisions and created negative feelings for many students who took years to finally realize that they were not deficient because of their belief or nonbelief.

Those days are gone and should be kept a part of America's past, not resurrected to add more division to our already fragmented society.

"Our highest court [is] cracking the whip, working to drive religious expression out of the public schools."

Restrictions on School Prayer Are Unfair to Students

Bill Murchison

In the 1962 case *Engel v. Vitale*, the Supreme Court ruled that teacher-led prayers in school classes violated the First Amendment's prohibition of an "establishment of religion." Since then the issue of school prayer has returned to the Supreme Court several times. In June 2000, the Supreme Court considered a Texas school district's proposal for beginning school football games with an invocation (that may or may not incorporate a prayer) by a student selected by other students. The Court ruled that such a practice constituted a constitutionally unacceptable version of school prayer. In the following viewpoint, Bill Murchison criticizes the Supreme Court for placing restrictions on school prayer, arguing that such rulings have unfairly limited the rights of students to religious expression, and that local communities and school boards should make school prayer decisions. Murchison is a conservative columnist for the *Dallas Morning News*.

As you read, consider the following questions:
1. Why do the country's intellectual elite oppose school prayer, according to Murchison?
2. How does the author respond to the argument that school prayers may be offensive to some?
3. Why is school prayer a result of the "tyranny of the minority," according to Murchison?

Reprinted from "School Prayer—Tyranny of the Minority," by Bill Murchison, syndicated column, June 27, 2000, by permission of Bill Murchison and Creators Syndicate.

The Supreme Court wound up its June 2000 term with another swipe at "school prayer"—latest in a sequence commencing 38 years ago. Back to an appellate court the justices kicked a case in which Alabama is bidding for approval of student-initiated prayer at "compulsory or non-compulsory" public school activities.

Yes, by now we know where this is going, don't we?

Last week [June 19, 2000], the court rebuked, 6 to 3, the Santa Fe, Texas, independent school district for a similar view of what constitutes "official" prayer.

The high court said on that occasion: Never mind whether students themselves decide they want a message of some kind delivered before football games; never mind that no religious message is required.

"In this context," wrote Justice John Paul Stevens, speaking for the majority, "the members of the listening audience must perceive the pregame message as a public expression of the views of the majority of the student body delivered with the approval of the school administration. . . ."

Think about that, the justices said to the 11th Circuit Court of Appeals, which had upheld Alabama's not dissimilar policy on prayer. I think we can guess what result the thinking process will produce. Sorry, kids, prayer's off.

Driving Out Religious Expression

Here we go again: our highest court cracking the whip, working to drive religious expression out of the public schools, as well as from other public venues. A pretty good job the justices are doing (despite some clean-up work needed in their own habitat; e.g., the cry that routinely opens court sessions—"God save the United States and this honorable Court.")

You ask why: Didn't the founders of the republic make clear enough their commitment to religion as a cornerstone of the virtuous community? Yeah, well, they did. Here's what it comes down to: That was then, this is now. We're changing the rules, see? Old rules are out; new ones are in.

The reason for the perdurability of the new rules is the support they enjoy from the country's intellectual elite, which is overwhelmingly secular in spirit. Supporters of this regime really don't care about antique abstractions like "divine authority." Not especially religious themselves, our intellectual elite—concentrated in the media and the professoriate—dislikes the idea of Godly intrusions in human affairs. The irrelevance—at best, the marginal relevance—of God is their gospel: God as just another intellectual possibility.

Reprinted by permission of Chuck Asay and Creators Syndicate.

And we don't force mere "possibilities" on others, do we? Oh, of course not—the moral equivalence of all ideas about sexuality; the utility of condoms; the sinfulness of "racism" and "sexism." We wouldn't let anything like that be propounded in the public schools, would we? Naw, not for a minute.

But invocation of the divine—that's different. It flies in the face of our cultural presuppositions! Offense might be taken!

Three Points

A few points here:

- Has anyone ever heard a pregame prayer? I have. Used to hear them all the time, in the '50s, at Corsicana High School football games. Guess what they prayed for over the P.A. system? America's conversion to the regimen of the First Methodist Church? Not a chance. Rather, for a clean game, and for the safe return of all fans to their homes. Gosh! What dangerous stuff! Likely to result in the overthrow of civilization! I'll bet the genre (where not squashed completely) hasn't changed much.

- On the someone-might-be-offended argument: Someone always gets offended. In the case of a pregame prayer, the village atheist, or a member of a different religion, or just some crank. Such is the price of our common life. I get offended myself: by the casual use of raw language in popular entertainment; by the wanton destruction of an old building; by shorts and tank tops on airplanes. You could make a federal, interstate-commerce-based case for the outlawing of such horrors. But to what end? Should the government, and, worse, the lawyers, run our collective life? In a free country we put up with a lot because putting up with particular things is the price of freedom.

- Local people can work these things out—as the people of Santa Fe, Texas, and of the State of Alabama have attempted to work them out. America isn't organized on the "one size fits all" principle, as the Supreme Court seems to believe. We elect local school boards to judge community needs; then we submit those judgments to the majority's will. If prayer becomes a deeply divisive issue for a community, the board can either stop the praying or figure out something that works.

Yes, the "tyranny of the majority" is a legitimate fear in any democracy. That isn't what goes on in the matter of school prayer. Right now the "tyranny of the minority" is the problem—one abetted by the tiniest of minorities, seated on that honorable court they pray so earnestly for God to save.

*"Posting the Ten Commandments in school
. . . would nudge toward God an unknown
number of youngsters who might otherwise
become moral monsters."*

Schools Should Post the Ten Commandments to Teach Morality

William Rusher

In the 1980 case of *Stone v. Graham*, the Supreme Court ruled that the posting of the Ten Commandments (the rules that, according to Jewish and Christian belief, were given by God to Moses) violated the Constitution's requirement of church-state separation. However, following the April 1999 violence at Columbine High School in Colorado, in which two students armed with automatic weapons killed thirteen people and wounded twenty-three before taking their own lives, many political and religious leaders called for the display of the Ten Commandments in schools and other public buildings. In the following viewpoint, conservative columnist William Rusher argues that displaying the Ten Commandments would expose students to the idea that God exists and has created rules for human conduct, thereby preventing repetitions of the Columbine massacre.

As you read, consider the following questions:
1. What does Rusher consider to be a stupid question?
2. Did America's founding fathers acknowledge God's existence, according to Rusher?

Reprinted from "What Can God's Ten Rules Do?" by William Rusher, *Conservative Chronicle*, September 8, 1999. Reprinted with permission from Newspaper Enterprise Association.

On NBC's *Today* show, co-host Katie Couric was questioning conservative Janet Parshall, and the conversation got around to whether the Ten Commandments ought to be posted in public schools. Ms. Parshall thought they should.

Whereupon Ms. Couric moved in for the kill: "But do you really think a simple posting of the Ten Commandments will prevent youth violence?"

A Stupid Question

That question is a belated but formidable entry in the competition for Stupidest Question of the 20th Century.

Nobody—certainly not Ms. Parshall nor I—is suggesting that if Eric Harris and Dylan Klebold, upon entering Columbine High School with their sawed-off shotguns under their coats, had happened to see the Ten Commandments posted on a wall and read the firm injunction "Thou shalt not kill," they would have turned on their heels and slunk away. Since they wouldn't, to suppose that this demonstrates the futility of the Ten Commandments is almost unbelievably absurd.

The truth is, however, that posting the Ten Commandments would inevitably give rise to a train of thought, among the student body as a whole and over a long period of time, so powerful in its implications that the proposal is being fought bitterly by people who reject those implications. If the Ten Commandments were really so innocuous, they wouldn't bother.

What, then, are those implications? The Ten Commandments are, or purport to be, commandments of God, given by him to Moses and transmitted by Moses to the people of Israel. If so, that necessarily implies two extremely important things: First, that there is a God, a Supreme Being who created heaven and earth and everything in them (including mankind); and second, that God has solemnly ordered mankind to obey the injunctions laid down in the commandments he gave to Moses.

If those commandments were posted prominently in every public school, their first effect would be to let the students know that the school authorities (and for that matter, the state government that controls them) acknowledges the existence of God. And their second effect would be to inform the students of God's 10 rules laid down to govern their behavior.

Further reflection would inevitably suggest to the students that disobeying the orders of a Supreme Being is rather obviously a bad idea. Unfortunate consequences are pretty clearly implied.

The Ten Commandments and Violence

The sheer brilliance of the Ten Commandments is that they codify, in a handful of words, acceptable human behavior. Not just for then—or now—but for all time. Language evolves, power shifts from nation to nation, messages are transmitted with the speed of light. Man erases one frontier after another, and yet we and our behavior—and the Commandments which govern that behavior—remain the same.

In 1999, Americans have been horrified to see violence spread from our city streets. "See you at the pole" worship services have been sprayed with gunfire. Young Christians, among others, at Columbine High School were murdered. One of the killers put his worldview this way: "My belief is that if I say something, it goes. I am the law. Feel no remorse, no sense of shame."

There is no better way to remind people that they are not the law, that God gives us the law, than publicly to post the Ten Commandments. A thousand courses in self-esteem cannot compensate for a failure to teach that simple truth. In fact, without acknowledging that God gives us life, liberty and law, it is positively dangerous to teach youngsters such as the Columbine killers to esteem only themselves.

Janet Parshall, *Insight*, December 6, 1999.

One can see why people who deny the existence of God, and of immutable moral "commandments," would fight the posting of the Ten Commandments with tooth and claw. They insist that this would violate the First Amendment's ban on the establishment of a state religion, though the statements of the Founding Fathers, beginning with the words of the Declaration of Independence, openly acknowledge the existence of God.

Once the subversive notion that there is a God, and that he has given us rules to obey and live by, begins to spread through the student population, its consequences over time are bound to be enormous. To some students, who have received religious instruction at home, it will be old news. Others, already steeped in secularism, will dismiss it as a bad joke. But many students, who have received little or no religious instruction from their parents, will note the respect with which society at large (as represented by the school) treats the Ten Commandments, and feel subtly drawn to the whole concept. Many will find it the door to a more wholesome life.

Simply posting the Ten Commandments in school will never wipe out sin. But it is a safe bet that it would nudge toward God an unknown number of youngsters who might otherwise become moral monsters not far different from the killers of Columbine High.

| "The idea that Ten Commandments on walls will change minds and hearts is naive and ill-advised."

Schools Should Not Post the Ten Commandments to Teach Morality

Lloyd Omdahl

Lloyd Omdahl is a professor of political science at the University of North Dakota and former lieutenant governor of that state. In the following viewpoint, he argues against posting the Ten Commandments in public places (including public schools), a practice that has been promoted by members of Congress and others in the wake of the April 1999 massacre at Columbine High School in Colorado. Omdahl asserts that such an action by itself would do little to prevent violence or teach character, but would violate the separation of church and state. In addition, he argues that Christians such as himself should object to the posting of the Ten Commandments because they misrepresent what he believes to be the true nature of Christianity.

As you read, consider the following questions:

1. What role do parents have in preventing school violence, according to Omdahl?
2. Why should Christians support the separation of church and state, according to the author?
3. How does Omdahl believe Christianity is misrepresented by the public posting of the Ten Commandments?

Reprinted, with permission, from "Evangelicals Should Be Champions, Not Critics, of Church-State Separation," by Lloyd Omdahl, on The Baptist Joint Committee website found at www.bjcpa.org/new2.html (as downloaded 8/17/00).

To deflect the clamor for more gun control after the Colorado school massacre, the U.S. House of Representatives passed an amendment declaring that the Tenth Amendment of the Constitution permits the posting of the Ten Commandments on public property, especially schools. . . . Since it constitutes a religious act, it warrants a theological response from at least one point of view.

If this provision stays in the final measure, the printing presses will start rolling with various translations of the Ten Commandments. Religious leaders, including my fellow evangelicals, will show up at school board meetings to advocate posting as a cure-all for violence in the schools. But the idea that Ten Commandments on walls will change minds and hearts is naive and ill-advised for a number of reasons.

A Token Action

First, this token action will misdirect appropriate responses to violence by taking the pressure off parents who must assume responsibility for the behavior of their children. If kids lack moral character when they reach school, there is very little that the school can do to significantly remedy the damage. Character is homemade.

Second, the Congress doesn't have the authority to interpret the Constitution, and the posting of the Ten Commandments is a violation of my First Amendment right to freedom of religion. This is the amendment that was first advocated by evangelical Christians, who won the crucial support of Thomas Jefferson and James Madison because evangelicals were being victimized by the state churches of the day. Without separation of church and state, the discrimination against evangelical Christians would have continued for decades after the adoption of the Constitution.

Evangelical Christians should be the champions—and not the critics—of the First Amendment requirement for separation of church and state. When the chips are down, we are still a minority in the United States and may well need the protection of the First Amendment down the road.

Third, official posting of the Ten Commandments not only violates the religious beliefs of certain minorities in society but, as far as I am concerned, it also obfuscates the real

meaning of New Testament Christianity. Government na-
tionalization of the Ten Commandments promoted the
heretical idea that civic religion and Christian faith are
somewhat synonymous. From my evangelical perspective,
Christianity cannot be nationalized or even institutionalized.

No Evidence for the Ten Commandments

Posting the Ten Commandments is supposed to change
people's behavior. Teens will stop shooting teens. Drug abuse
will wane. This is an empirical claim that can be tested scientifically. Trouble is, there is no evidence at all for this
claim. Commandment supporters say that, when prayer and
Bible-reading were in the schools, morality was higher and
crime was lower. Critics reply that, when God was in the
schools, racism and gang wars were up and tolerance for religious minorities was down. Fact is, such correlations are
not well established, if at all. And even if they were, correlations are not the same thing as cause and effect. If they were,
we could plausibly claim that religion causes school shootings since most of the recent high-profile school shootings
involved assailants who were religious.

Worse still, posting the Ten Commandments in school is
likely to *cause* conflict because they are partisan. There are
several versions—Protestant, Catholic, and others—each
based on a different dogma. There is no "standard" version.
. . . Whose version should get posted? Fight! Fight!

Lewis Vaughn, *Free Inquiry*, Fall 1999.

It is my view that anybody who knows and understands
the New Testament also knows and understands that being a
Christian is a commitment of faith that cannot be made for
a person by the government, the Elks, the school district or
a church.

Furthermore, the posting of the Ten Commandments in
a secular society violates my belief that becoming a Christian
begins first with repentance, then faith in Jesus Christ and
then obedience. Without personal repentance and faith,
obedience to the Ten Commandments posted on the school-
room walls is meaningless.

By aggressively promoting the Ten Commandments,
evangelical Christians are conveying the impression to nonbelievers and nonevangelical Christians that Christianity

consists of rules and regulations without reference to the prerequisites of repentance and faith.

For the infinitesimal good that the posting of the Ten Commandments would do, it is hardly worth shifting the responsibility for morals from parents, adding to the credibility of civil religion, violating the Constitution and misrepresenting Christianity. The First Amendment should protect my right to pursue Christian evangelism without the government confusing the theological issues involved.

Periodical Bibliography

The following articles have been selected to supplement the diverse views presented in this chapter. Addresses are provided for periodicals not indexed in the *Readers' Guide to Periodical Literature*, the *Alternative Press Index*, the *Social Sciences Index*, or the *Index to Legal Periodicals and Books*.

America	"Public Schools and Religion," January 15–22, 2000.
Eric Buehrer and Edd Doerr	"Symposium: Should Public Schools Celebrate Thanksgiving and Christmas Holidays?" *Insight*, December 2, 1996. Available from 3600 New York Ave. NE, Washington, DC 20002.
Christian Century	"New Church-School Guidelines," January 5–12, 2000.
Christianity Today	"Hang Ten?" March 6, 2000.
Edd Doerr	"Bible and School," *Humanist*, January/February 2000.
Thomas W. Flynn	"The Case for Affirmative Secularism," *Free Inquiry*, Spring 1996. Available from PO Box 664, Amherst, NY 14226-0664.
Michael J. Gerson	"Public Schools Teach Bible as History," *U.S. News & World Report*, January 12, 1998.
Mark Kellner	"Back to the Bible," *Christianity Today*, September 4, 2000.
Charles Krauthammer	"The Real Message of Creationism," *Time*, November 22, 1999.
Ben Marcus	"Praise the Lord and Pass the Football," *Time*, July 10, 2000.
Barbara McEwan	"Public Schools, Religion, and Public Responsibility," *USA Today*, May 1997.
Janet Parshall and Jerrold Nadler	"Symposium: Is It a Good Idea to Post the Ten Commandments in Public Buildings?" *Insight*, December 6, 1999.
Alan Singer	"Separation of Church and State Protects Both Secular and Religious Worlds," *Phi Delta Kappan*, February 2000.
Lewis Vaughn	"Protect My Children from the Ten Commandments," *Free Inquiry*, Fall 1999.
George F. Will	"The Censoring of Zachary," *Newsweek*, March 20, 2000.
World & I	"Special Report: Faith in Our Schools," December 1999.

For Further Discussion

Chapter 1

1. What do the authors of the Summit Ministries viewpoint mean when they argue that the United States is a Christian nation? Is this different from arguing that the United States is a religious nation? Explain your answer.

2. What different interpretations do Mark Weldon Whitten and the authors connected with Summit Ministries make about the First Amendment? What arguments and evidence do they use to back their views? Who, in your opinion, offers a more plausible interpretation?

3. What "conventional yardsticks" does Kenneth D. Wald use to measure religious commitment in America? In your view, are these adequate tools for answering the question of whether Americans are a religious people? Why or why not?

4. What criticisms does Jeremiah Creedon describe of the "cafeteria" approach to spirituality? Do you agree or disagree with them? Explain.

5. Both Marvin Olasky and Alan Dershowitz provide examples of discrimination or prejudice in support of their views. Can you think of examples of discrimination from your own experience or those of people you know that coincide with the arguments of either Olasky or Dershowitz? Explain.

Chapter 2

1. What evidence does Patrick F. Fagan marshal to support his contention that religion is a beneficial force? Does he offer convincing proof of his claim? Give examples to support your answer.

2. What positive defense does Wendy Kaminer make of atheism? Does this contradict the views put forth by Fagan? Explain.

3. What examples does Joe Loconte give of the work of religious organizations? Do these examples provide an adequate response to questions raised by Jacob Hacker? Why or why not?

4. What constitutional objections does the Anti-Defamation League make about "Charitable Choice" legislation? Are any of these objections directly addressed by John Ashcroft? After reading the viewpoints, do you believe that government funding of religious groups violates the separation of church and state? Explain your answers.

Chapter 3

1. After reading the arguments of Marc D. Stern and Christopher L. Eisgruber/Lawrence G. Sager, do you believe religious practices should receive exemptions from laws such as workplace discrimination rules or zoning regulations? Is this an issue in which compromise is possible, in your view? Explain.

2. Why is the issue of refusing medical care for religious reasons more troublesome when children are involved? After reading the arguments of Rita Swan and Stephen L. Carter, do you think parents' religious beliefs should be ignored when it comes to medical treatment of children? Why or why not?

3. Why can Christians serve in the military with Muslims and Jews, but not Wiccans, according to Robert L. Maginnis? Can one reasonably make a distinction between "minority" religions and "fringe" religions, in your opinion? Why or why not?

4. Does Chad Anctil leave you with a much different picture of the Wiccan religion than Maginnis? Which portrayal do you find more convincing? What arguments does he make regarding Wicca and his own fitness to serve?

Chapter 4

1. Warren A. Nord asserts that ignoring religion in education betrays a hostility to religion. Do you agree or disagree? Does Edd Doerr betray a "hostility to religion" in his arguments, in your view? Explain.

2. Bill Murchison blames the "intellectual elite" for removing prayer from public schools. Is this choice of words objectively descriptive, in your opinion? Explain.

3. Most of the recent school prayer cases have revolved around student-led prayers at football games and convocations, rather than classroom prayers such as those described by Jeff Archer. Do the same points Archer makes about teacher-led prayers apply to student-led prayers, in your opinion? Why or why not?

4. What scenario regarding Eric Harris and Dylan Klebold does Rusher describe? What point is he making about opponents of posting the Ten Commandments? Do you agree or disagree with his assessment of what posting the Ten Commandments could accomplish? Explain.

5. Does the fact that Lloyd Omdahl is a professed Christian lend more or less credence to his arguments concerning the posting of the Ten Commandments, in your opinion? Explain.

Organizations to Contact

The editors have compiled the following list of organizations concerned with the issues debated in this book. The descriptions are derived from materials provided by the organizations. All have publications or information available for interested readers. The list was compiled on the date of publication of the present volume; the information provided here may change. Be aware that many organizations take several weeks or longer to respond to inquiries, so allow as much time as possible.

American Atheists
PO Box 5733, Parsippany, NJ 07054-6733
(908) 276-7300 • fax: (908) 276-7402
e-mail: info@atheists.org • website: www.atheists.org

American Atheists is an educational organization dedicated to the complete and absolute separation of church and state. It opposes religious involvement such as prayer and religious clubs in public schools. The organization's purpose is to stimulate freedom of thought and inquiry concerning religious beliefs and practices. It publishes the monthly *American Atheist Newsletter*.

American Center for Law and Justice (ACLJ)
PO Box 64429,Virginia Beach, VA 23467
(757) 226-2489 • fax: (757) 226-2836
e-mail: aclj@exis.net • website: www.aclj.org

The center is a public interest law firm and educational organization dedicated to promoting liberty, life, and the family. ACLJ provides legal services and support to attorneys and others who are involved in defending the religious and civil liberties of Americans. It publishes the booklets *Students' Rights and the Public Schools* and *Taking the Gospel to the Streets: Your Rights to Preach the Good News in Public Places*.

American Civil Liberties Union (ACLU)
125 Broad St., 18th Floor, New York, NY 10004
(212) 549-2500 • fax: (212) 549-2646
website: www.aclu.org

The ACLU is a national organization that works to defend Americans' civil rights as guaranteed by the U.S. Constitution, including rights of religious expression. It opposes excessive entanglement of church and state. Its publications include the handbook *The Right to Religious Liberty* and the semiannual newsletter *Civil Liberties Alert*.

Americans for Religious Liberty (ARL)
PO Box 6656, Silver Spring, MD 20916
(301) 598-2447
website: www.infidels.org/~ltaylor/arl.html
ARL is an educational organization that works to preserve religious, intellectual, and personal freedom in a secular democracy. It advocates the strict separation of church and state. ARL publishes numerous pamphlets on church/state issues and the quarterly newsletter *Voice of Reason*.

Americans United for Separation of Church and State (AUSCS)
1816 Jefferson Pl. NW, Washington, DC 20036
(202) 466-3234 • fax: (202) 466-2587
e-mail: americansunited@au.org • website: www.au.org
AUSCS works to protect religious freedom for all Americans. Its principal means of action are litigation, education, and advocacy. It opposes the passing of either federal or state laws that threaten the separation of church and state. Its publications include brochures, pamphlets, and the monthly newsletter *Church and State*.

American Vision
3150-A Florence Rd. SW, Suite 2, Powder Springs, GA 30127
(770) 222-7266 • fax: (770) 222-7269
e-mail: avpress@mindspring.com
website: www.americanvision.org
American Vision is a Christian educational organization working to build a Christian civilization. It believes the Bible ought to be applied to every area of life, including government. American Vision publishes the monthly newsletter *Biblical Worldview*.

Christian Coalition (CC)
1801-L Sara Dr., Chesapeake, VA 23320
(804) 424-2630 • fax: (804) 434-9068
e-mail: coalition@cc.org • website: www.cc.org
Founded by evangelist Pat Robertson, the coalition is a grassroots political organization working to stop what it believes is the moral decay of government. Its publications include the monthly newsletter *The Religious Right Watch* and the monthly tabloid *Christian American*.

Council for Secular Humanism
PO Box 664, Amherst, NY 14226-0664
(716) 636-7571 • fax: (716) 636-1733
e-mail: info@SecularHumanism.org
website: www.secularhumanism.org

The council is an educational organization dedicated to fostering the growth of democracy, secular humanism, and the principles of free inquiry. It publishes the magazine *Free Inquiry*.

Eagle Forum
PO Box 618, Alton, IL 62002
(618) 462-5415 • fax: (618) 462-8909
e-mail: eagle@eagleforum.org • website: www.eagleforum.org

Eagle Forum is a Christian group that promotes morality and traditional family values as revealed through the Bible. It opposes many facets of public education and liberal government. The forum publishes the monthly *Phyllis Schlafly Report* and a periodic newsletter.

The Heritage Foundation
214 Massachusetts Ave. NE, Washington, DC 20002-4999
(202) 546-4400 • (800) 544-4843 • fax: (202) 544-6979
e-mail: pubs@heritage.org • website: www.heritage.org

The Heritage Foundation is a conservative public policy research institute that advocates traditional American values, free-market economics and limited government. It occasionally publishes articles on religion in American life in its publications, which include the monthly *Policy Review*.

Interfaith Alliance
1012 14th St. NW, Washington, DC 20005
(202) 639-6370 • fax: (202) 639-6375
e-mail: tia@tialliance.org • website: www.tialliance.org

The alliance is a nonpartisan organization that advances a mainstream, faith-based political agenda. Its members, who represent more than fifty faith traditions, promote religion as a healing and constructive force in public life. It publishes the *Light*, a quarterly newsletter.

Ontario Consultants on Religious Tolerance (OCRT)
PO Box 514, Wellesley Island, NY 13640-0514
fax: (613) 547-9015
e-mail: ocrt_qu@cgo.wave.ca • website: www.religioustolerance.org

OCRT is a private organization that believes in the fundamental importance of religious tolerance in the protection of civil rights.

Its website has numerous articles and essays on various religions and their beliefs, especially minority religions in the United States and Canada. It also provides articles on issues such as abortion, euthanasia, and religious discrimination.

People for the American Way (PFAW)
2000 M St. NW, Suite 400, Washington, DC 20036
(202) 467-4999 • fax: (202) 293-2672
e-mail: pfaw@pfaw.org • website: www.pfaw.org

PFAW works to increase tolerance and respect for America's diverse cultures, religions, and values such as freedom of expression. It distributes educational materials, leaflets, and brochures, including reports on activities of religious right organizations.

The Pluralism Project
Harvard University, 201 Vanserg Hall, 25 Francis Ave.,
Cambridge, MA 02138
e-mail: staff@pluralism.org • website: www.pluralism.org

The Pluralism Project was founded by Harvard University professor Diana L. Eck to study and document the growing religious diversity in the United States, with a special focus on immigrant religious communities. It publishes a CD-ROM *On Common Ground: World Religions in America*, and furnishes articles and other information on its website.

Religion in Public Education Resource Center (RPERC)
5 County Center Dr., Oroville, CA 95965
(916) 538-7847 • fax: (916) 538-7846
e-mail: bbenoit@edison.bcoe.butte.k12.ca.us
website: www.csuchico.edu/rs/rperc.html

The center believes religion should be studied in public schools in ways that do not promote the values or beliefs of one religion over another. It publishes the triannual magazine *Religion and Public Education* and resource materials for teachers and administrators.

Rockford Institute
934 N. Main St., Rockford, IL 61103-7061
(815) 964-5811 • fax: (815) 965-1826
website: www.rockfordinstitute.org

The institute works to return America to Judeo-Christian values and supports traditional roles for men and women. Its Center on Religion and Society advocates a more public role for religion and religious values in American life. The institute's publications include the monthly periodical *Family in America*, the monthly *Reli-*

gion & Society Report, and the quarterly newsletter *Main Street Memorandum*.

Toward Tradition

PO Box 58, Mercer Island, WA 98040
(800) 591-7579
www.towardtradition.org

Toward Tradition is a national educational movement of Jews and Christians and other Americans seeking to advance the nation toward traditional, faith-based, American principles of constitutional and limited government, the rule of law, representative democracy, free markets, a strong military, and a moral public culture. It disseminates position papers from its website and distributes a newsletter.

Bibliography of Books

Helen A. Berger — *A Community of Witches: Contemporary Neo-Paganism and Witchcraft in the United States.* Columbia: University of South Carolina Press, 1999.

John H. Berthwrong — *The Divine Deli: Religious Identity in the North American Cultural Mosaic.* Maryknoll, NY: Orbis, 1999.

Brian Edward Brown — *Religion, Law, and the Land: Native Americans and the Judicial Interpretation of Native Land.* Westport, CT: Greenwood Press, 1999.

Tony Campolo — *Revolution and Renewal: How Churches Are Saving Our Cities.* Louisville, KY: Westminster John Knox Press, 2000.

Stephen L. Carter — *God's Name in Vain: The Wrongs and Rights of Religion in Politics.* New York: BasicBooks, 2000.

Richard Cimino and Don Lattin — *Shopping for Faith: American Religion in the New Millennium.* San Francisco: Jossey-Bass, 1998.

Julia Mitchell Corbett — *Religion in America.* Englewood Cliffs, NJ: Prentice-Hall, 1999.

Lorne L. Dawson, ed. — *Cults in Context: Readings in the Study of New Religious Movements.* New Brunswick, NJ: Transaction, 1998.

John J. DiIulio Jr., ed. — *What's God Got to Do with the American Experiment?: Essays on Religion and Politics.* Washington, DC: Brookings Institution, 2000.

Eldon J. Eisenach — *The Next Religious Establishment.* Lanham, MD: Rowman & Littlefield, 2000.

Robert S. Ellwood and Harry Partin — *Religious and Spiritual Groups in Modern America.* Englewood Cliffs, NJ: Prentice-Hall, 1996.

Richard W. Flory and Donald E. Miller, eds. — *GenX Religion.* New York: Routledge, 2000.

Bruce David Forbes and Jeffrey H. Mahan, eds. — *Religion and Popular Culture in America.* Berkeley: University of California Press, 2000.

Robert Booth Fowler et al. — *Religion and Politics in America: Faith, Culture, and Strategic Choices.* Boulder, CO: Westview, 1999.

Winifred Gallagher — *Working on God.* New York: Random House, 1999.

Alex Heard — *Apocalypse Pretty Soon: Travels in End-Time America.* New York: Doubleday, 2000.

| Hugh Hewitt | *Searching for God in America*. Nashville, TN: Word Publishing, 1996. |

| Martin E. Marty with Jonathan Moore | *Politics, Religion, and the Common Good*. San Francisco: Jossey-Bass, 2000. |

| Eric Michael Mazur | *The Americanization of Religious Minorities: Confronting the Constitutional Order*. Baltimore: Johns Hopkins University Press, 1999. |

| J. Gordon Melton | *The Encyclopedia of American Religions*. Detroit: MI: Gale Research, 1996. |

| Timothy Miller, ed. | *America's Alternative Religions*. Albany, NY: SUNY Press, 1995. |

| Jacob Neusner, ed. | *World Religions in America: An Introduction*. Louisville, KY: Westminster John Knox Press, 1999. |

| Steve Rabey | *In Search of Authentic Faith: How Emerging Generations Are Transforming the Church*. Colorado Springs, CO: Waterbrook, 2001. |

| Frank Spencer Read, revised by Samuel S. Hill | *Handbook of Denominations in the United States*. Nashville, TN: Abingdon, 1997. |

| Ralph Reed | *Active Faith: How Christians Are Changing the Soul of American Politics*. New York: Free Press, 1996. |

| Wade Clark Roof | *Spiritual Marketplace: Baby Boomers and the Remaking of American Religion*. Princeton, NJ: Princeton University Press, 1999. |

| John K. Roth | *Private Needs, Public Selves: Talk About Religion in America*. Urbana: University of Illinois Press, 1997. |

| Martin S. Sheffer | *God Versus Caesar: Belief, Worship, and Proselytizing Under the First Amendment*. Albany, NY: SUNY Press, 1999. |

| Christian Smith | *Christian America? What Evangelicals Really Want*. Berkeley: University of California Press, 2000. |

| Jeff Spinner-Halev | *Surviving Diversity: Religion and Democratic Citizenship*. Baltimore: Johns Hopkins University Press, 2000. |

| James D. Tabor and Eugene V. Gallagher | *Why Waco?: Cults and the Battle for Religious Freedom in America*. Berkeley: University of California Press, 1995. |

| Ronald F. Thiemann | *Religion in Public Life: A Dilemma for Democracy*. Washington, DC: Georgetown University Press, 1996. |

Cal Thomas and Ed Dobson	*Blinded by Might: Can the Religious Right Save America?* Grand Rapids, MI: Zondervan, 1999.
Steve Wall	*Dancing with God: Americans Who Have Been Touched by the Divine.* New York: St. Martin's Press, 1999.
Jim Wallis	*Faith Works: Lessons from the Life of an Activist Preacher.* New York: Random House, 2000.
Clyde Wilcox	*Onward Christian Soldiers.* Boulder, CO: Westview, 2000.
Stuart A. Wright, ed.	*Armageddon in Waco: Critical Perspectives on the Branch Davidian Conflict.* Chicago: University of Chicago Press, 1995.

Index

agnosticism. *See* nonbelievers
alcohol abuse, 64
Alcoholics Anonymous, 64
American Academy of
    Pediatricians, 145
Amish, the, 129, 152
Anctil, Chad, 162
Anti-Defamation League, 15, 99
Archer, Jeff, 185
Ashcroft, John, 93
Asian religions, 41
Asser, Seth, 143
atheism
    and morality, 73–74
    see also nonbelievers
Azusa Christian Community, 89

baby boomers, 43–44
Barna, George, 41, 43
Barr, Bob, 156, 157, 159
Barton, David, 26
Beasley, David, 77
Berthrong, John H., 41–42, 44–45
Bible, 33
Bill of Rights. *See* First
    Amendment
births, out of wedlock, 62
Bishop, George, 18
Bishop, Sanford, 113
Black, Hugo, 176
Boston, Rob, 102
Brennan, William, 184
Britton, Milton, 85
Buddhism, 41
Bush, George W.
    on Charitable Choice, 59
    and faith-based organizations,
        79, 82

Campus Crusade, 180
Cancellaro, Louis A., 65–66
Capps, Walter, 121
Carter, Jimmy, 54
Carter, Stephen L., 150
Catholic Charities, 32, 78, 92, 101
Charitable Choice, 59
    expanding, 95–97
        support for, 97–98, 100
    inspiring examples of, 95

is bad for religion, 103–104
is bad public policy, 103
is unconstitutional, 101–103
Charitable Choice Expansion Act
    (1998), 95–98
Chaves, Mark, 19
children. *See* medical care,
    withholding
Christianity
    American support for, 35
    censored in public schools, 21
    customized forms of, 41–42
    military service members
        identifying with, 157
    negative view of
        faith-based organizations
            influenced by, 47–48
        international influence of, 47
        manifestations of, 48–51
    nonpreferential aid to, 28
    religious freedom amendment
        benefiting, 120–21
Christian Science church, 143
    beliefs of, 146
    children's deaths in, 147–48, 151
    effectiveness of spiritual healing
        in, 153
    as health care system, 147
    informing state authorities on
        treatments by, 153–54
    response to pediatricians by, 145
Christophobia, 48–51
churches
    attendance, 18–19, 32–33
        and crime, 79
        and depression, 66
        as influencing prosperity, 63–64
        and suicide rate, 66
    membership of, 31–32
    money contributed to, 32
    number of, 31
    see also faith-based organizations
Church of the First Born, 143
church-state separation
    in First Amendment, 21–22,
        28–29
    and government funding for
        faith-based organizations, 59
    is a constitutional assumption,